THE
VISIBLE
WOMAN

THE
VISIBLE
WOMAN

MORE LUST, LESS MUST

HOW THE OLDER WOMAN CAN START
FEELING VISIBLE AGAIN,
REKINDLE HER PASSION FOR LIFE
AND
START HER NEXT ADVENTURE

IRENE BRANKIN

A Wise Woman = a truth-teller; a woman
of age and wisdom.

Wisdom = the thoughtful application
of learning.

www.irenebrankin.co.uk

First published in Great Britain 2011 by Lydhar Press,14 Lynton Road, Hadleigh, Essex. SS7 2QQ

A CIP catalogue record for this book is available from the British Library

ISBN – 978-0-9569265-0-0

Text and Cover Design by Two Associates

Printed and bound in Great Britain by MPG Biddles Ltd, 24 Rollesby Road, Harwick Industrial Estate, King's Lynn, Norfolk PE30 4LS

About the Author

Irene Brankin has worked in the field of personal development for over 30 years. She is an established Chartered Counselling Psychologist, Personal Coach, Supervisor and Group Facilitator who has worked in the UK and on the Continent. She brings many years of personal and professional experience to her work, together with a wry sense of Glaswegian humour.

Mother of one son and grandmother to two little ones; Irene is an enthusiastic woman who enjoys the rainbow of life and won't sit quietly on the sidelines. She is of the "Been there, done that, got the T-shirt" generation and knows the triumphs, pitfalls and waywardness of being alive. She has had cancer and is lucky enough to still be standing and living life to the full. She has experienced the stresses and strains of being a director of a training organisation; of changing careers; of coping with family illness; and of juggling too many and too few balls. The basis of Irene's work is to enable people to appreciate and believe in themselves as well as to rekindle their passion for life.

Contents

Acknowledgements

I am indebted to my wonderful literary agent, Jacqueline Burns, who pushed and prodded me with her suggestions and whose editing skills enhanced the manuscript; to the talented book cover designer, David Eldridge, and also the clever copy editor, Emma Rose. Thanks also to Suzy Greaves who gave me my original nudge in this direction. And to Helen and Janet for reading all the manuscript and for offering their wise advice.

A very big thank you to:

My husband Eddie whose patience whilst I have been on the computer is beyond compare – mind you he had peace and quiet for his football and golf!

My son Ian and daughter-in-law Louise – I told you I was writing a book! I am so proud of you Ian for being our son and for all you've achieved, particularly in being such a good Dad. Louise, you are a wonderful Mother to our grandchildren and were so kind to me when I was ill – I'll never forget that.

Lydia – the most beautiful, intelligent and talented granddaughter who I love dearly.

Harry – the most charming, delightful and quick-witted wee boy who makes me laugh a lot.

My brother Harry and his wife Jean.

My lovely friends at the 'Fat Club' – Irene, Debbie, Lynn, Lin, Barbara, Jan, Viv for a good laugh and our teacher Cherie for keeping us on track.

To my lovely neighbours – especially Julie and June.

I am so grateful to my friends and colleagues from The Psycho-synthesis & Education Trust in London (amongst them Liz, Andrea, Angie, Brenda, Alannah, Brian, Anita, Marilyn, Ruth, and my teachers, Diana, Judith and Piero), and those at the Psykosyntesadakemin in Stockholm (Fredrik, Margareta, Maud, Mona, Gunilla, Malin, Py, Joanne, and new Director, Eva, with most especially Nina-Christina – you are a star) for the support, laughter, learning and joy of being in their company.

I also must mention all the participants of my courses and my clients and wonderful supervisees over the past 30 years – thank you.

To all the health professionals who helped me along the way especially my Pilates teacher, Marianne, Pauline and Jane, my trainer, who helped my body regain strength and most importantly, my wonderful Consultant, Neil Rothnie, together with the continuing kind support from Joanne Glover.

Also special thanks to Sharon for keeping me going when I was ill with a postcard every day! You live what you teach.

Maggie's Cancer Caring Centres for giving something that is so needed.

To the wonderful women who were willing to share their steps to being visible – Amarita, Ann, Anne, Carole, Carolina, Janet, Lynn, Kristina, Margaret, Marta, Sharon, and Sue. I can't thank you enough.

Foreword by Janet Ellis

In fairy tales, the middle-aged woman doesn't get much of a role. There are young girls in plenty and lots of toothless crones (or wicked stepmothers) but nothing in between. Real life, of course, is different. We're everywhere! And in the age of the Baby Boomer, there are more of us than ever. But in some ways, we're as invisible as in the story books.

In a way, it's a self-fulfilling prophecy- if women feel invisible, they don't call attention to themselves. And anyone- man or woman – will tell you that getting older has its trials and tribulations. It could be much easier to hide away, not cause a fuss, and not look in the mirror again.

Irene Brankin stands up and speaks out for her generation, and her message is: We're here! Yes we're older but we are a little wiser and with plenty of experiences to share. And the first person we need to convince is ourselves. This easy to follow guide is a travel book for the universe of the older woman. Getting to know and liberate your visible self is the best way to face a positive future, a future where we women can be seen and heard, proud to take up our proper place in the world.

London Centre Patron of Maggie's Cancer Caring Centres

Here's a quick test. If you answer 'yes' to 4 or more of the following then this book is for you.

Is This You ?

☐ Do you feel you're invisible?

☐ Have you stopped worrying about how you look?

☐ Do you wear drab colours?

☐ Do you feel overlooked?

☐ Do you feel boxed in because of your age?

☐ Does life feel grey?

☐ Do you believe you still have something to offer from your life's experience?

☐ Do you refuse to be invisible or fade into the shadows?

☐ Do you find you have no interest in anything new?

☐ Do you feel too young to 'hang up your spurs' or wear that crimpolene dress?

☐ Are you asking yourself 'what is my role now?'

☐ Are you not yet ready to give in or give up?

☐ Do you still want to celebrate yourself and life?

☐ Do you just need a push or a nudge to move on?

☐ Do you feel that life is worth living to the full?

☐ Do you believe that you can be of service to life?

☐ Do you find yourself asking, 'Is this all there is now?'

☐ Have you found yourself at a crossroads in life?

☐ Are you ready for your next adventure?

Introduction

Ageism is rife in our society, but particularly so for women. Once over the age of 50, we are portrayed as too old, past it, invisible and sometimes even replaceable, both at home and in the workplace. Women in the public eye are pushed out of jobs that a man is still deemed young enough to do. And ordinary women find themselves replaced with a younger model or pressured into erasing any evidence of ageing.

Perhaps fuelled by the media, our society is obsessed with youth. There are many theories about how this has come about. I'm not going to debate them here as that isn't the focus of my book. However, what I will say is that the underlying assumption of this obsession is that the normal process of ageing is somehow wrong and should be prevented or corrected at all cost. We only have to look at the 'beauty' treatments that attempt to halt the ageing process to know this. Some of them involving injecting poison into our bodies. And then there's the 'airbrushing' that allows celebrities to appear young and slim forever. The message is don't be yourself, don't be real; be this ideal woman or else you'll be invisible.

But this view ignores all the positive things about ageing. With age comes the ability to view life in an easier way. It brings wisdom, experience, life skills and maturity.

It's my sense of anger and frustration at this waste of wisdom and life experience that older women possess that inspired me to write *The Visible Woman*. We shouldn't accept this feeling of being put out to pasture as though we no longer have anything to offer society. It's time to rise up and challenge the myth of ageing.

I've talked to many women about how they feel about ageing, and one thing really stands out. There is an agreement that one of the worst things about ageing is becoming invisible.

There are two reasons why the older woman is treated as discounted and invisible:

1. Broadly speaking, the media portrays older women as being past their best, no longer desirable, and having little left to contribute.
2. We accept this view and even collude with it.

So it seems that youth is prized and age is devalued. My view is that to age is a given. It's natural- if we're lucky enough to get the chance to live long enough to age. And yet I know there is a certain unease at growing older which we cannot deny: those laughter lines we see in the mirror, everything drooping as the years go by, the problems with clothes – we can't find dresses with decent sleeves!

Yes, all the above is true and we need to remember that it's a two-way process. If you let society overlook you, they will. So how you experience age – gracefully or disgracefully is up to you even if you can celebrate how young you still look or feel.

Society doesn't have to just focus on the negative aspects of ageing. It can re-look and see that we are also developing with our life cycle. We can make use of our life experience, wisdom and our ability to laugh at the craziness of life. It is time to stand up for ourselves and acknowledge the positive qualities that come with this natural evolution.

We all want to be caught up in the ebb and flow of life; to be involved and to know that we matter and we still count. These basic human needs do not diminish with the years!

I wrote this book for the women who are the 'Been there, done that, got the "T-Shirt' generation. The resilient thrivers who now have more space, time and money to focus on themselves. Perhaps you are:

☐ at a crossroad in your personal and/or professional life

- [ ] a mother or grandmother who refuses to fade into the shadows
- [ ] an empty-nester or a career woman who is ready for their next adventure
- [ ] mature enough to laugh at life but you're stuck and need a kick up the backside to get going again
- [ ] feeling like you are going crazy
- [ ] feeling boxed in by ageism
- [ ] aware that life is worth living to the full but aren't doing it

If so, what are you going to do about it? Are you taking the risk of being visible and standing out? Or have you accepted that youth is where it's at and the best of your life is behind you? Are you fighting a feeling that keeps flitting in and out of your mind of being past it now that you are in the second half of your life? Have you become part of the furniture – not seen? Are you colluding with the 'You're over the hill at 50+' message?

It may be that in your working life, your role or title gave you a sense of identity, or a feeling of respect, and now that this has changed or is changing, you no longer know who you are any more. Or sometimes it's our sense of ourselves as sexual beings that has faded. Perhaps you are stuck and you feel like you're going nowhere, yet you know there is still much to be expressed. Others of you may feel that there is nothing wrong and you are not desperately unhappy, but there is a kind of staleness – your passion for life isn't there any more. You have a sense that there could be still more to come.

Women often say that as they age, they feel they don't know who they are any more. It is like their souls are crying out for some attention. You may be asking 'What has happened to that woman I used to know? Where did I go? When did I become invisible to myself and others? When did I switch off or become too busy to give space to me?' Stop a moment and see which applies to you right now.

In the first part of life, through our twenties, thirties and forties, we're usually busy trying to attain love and building self-esteem. This is achieved through our various roles in, for example, our family, career and status, and gives us a comfortable place in society. However, this is usually where life begins to go awry as we slowly disappear under the many roles we take on. *We not only take on these roles but we feel we are the role and only the role.*

Added to this, we're faced with a media which offers not only an ideal view of family life but also that only attractive women are to be seen. We take on the added pressure of how we 'must' be. For the most part, this is fine in the wider scheme of things but we have not given ourselves the 'me' time. The time to breathe into us before we forget who we are.

As we move into the second part of life though, it is time to wake-up. This is what I describe as the *Wake-up Call.* Mine was a dramatic one, a life-threatening, health scare, but they're not all like that. For many women, it is just the sense that life is flat and a bit dull and just not as enjoyable as it once was.

Your Call tells *you* that it is time to assimilate all of *your* life's experiences. It's time to see what it is you want to do with the rest of your life. You've probably forgotten just how much you've done with your life – your accomplishments and gifts that are so needed in the world today.

You are always being asked to honour who you truly are. To live a life that makes the most of your strengths. Return this request as your gift is precious, needed and yours to be shared and enjoyed. You can make a difference to those in your family and to generations to come. This is what's known as your legacy. Something was being asked of me once I regained my strength after my illness. And when

I returned the Call, this book became my legacy. Throughout the book, I am using *Call* interchangeable with *Wise Woman* - your inner wisdom, your inner sense of knowing, your intuition, the part of you that somehow knows what is right for you.

Remember that life will change when you return or respond to your Call. Even if you go through difficult times, you'll manage to handle the issues that come up better as you'll have more confidence in your life experience.

Yes, now is the time to start to value what you do have - your wisdom from your life experience, your eldership. Your maturity provides a new richness to your personality. Everything you have lived is grist to your mill and has made you who you are. It is now time to start the next phase of your life.

One chapter of the book of life may have closed but the next one could be infinitely better as you push the boundaries of what we once called middle age. You can be much bigger, or more at peace with yourself than you think you can be. There is a world of expansion and possibilities out there. So slow down and listen to your Wise Woman. This is the time to come home to yourself. You can consider others' opinions as well as your own, and then see that *you* do have choices. You've done your bit for others and now it is time for you.

To be really frank, when we don't spend enough time on ourselves, we are not as there for others as we might think. We fade and become invisible in all areas of our lives. Others do notice.

I know that the Visible Woman exercises in the book will be of great benefit to you. I encourage you to be curious as curiosity is an essential quality of aliveness. It's our passion for life. It's how we learn and grow, have adventures, discover what we like or dislike.

Each chapter will be about *You* – getting to know yourself better – thereby becoming more visible to yourself and eventually more visible to everyone else too. The response from the world will come to matter less – even with ageism so rife – even when you are ignored or overlooked you'll cope because you are more comfortable in your own skin and know your own worth. Let's face it, it's hard to ignore a woman who's truly aware of her power and is in charge of her destiny as much as life allows.

This book is a product of my wanting to share with you my insights and experiences as a woman as well as someone who dealt with cancer as a part of my own journey. I also wrote it from my perspective as a psychologist to help you to have more choice – inner freedom – in your life. It will enable you to look at the loss of energy when you are not being stretched enough. This loss of energy can lead to depression and cause you to overlook the fact that you still have so much to offer from your experience and wisdom to prevent yourself from fading away.

As you know, now is a time of much change and happenings in the world. One of them is that older women are listening to their passion. They know that it is their time to be visible with their wisdom and life experience. They are also listening to their inner rhythm of when to be out in the world and when it is time to be inward. Women are celebrating that Call to continue to connect to spirit as well as grounded work in the world.

Within each of us there is a Wise Woman who knows who she really is. Together we will find her. She's always there but you have been ignoring her Call. Until now.

Are you ready to listen to the Call of your inner Wise Woman? This is your time to relish and enjoy the next part of your life. Ready? Then turn the page.

How to Use This Book

On this exciting and thoughtful journey, I will ask you to do some exercises – the Visible Woman exercises. You can follow the steps or dip in and out as you need depending on where you are in your life. Or you can choose to return to them again and again to see how your responses change on different occasions.

Most of the exercises I am using come from my involvement in psychosynthesis, or have been adapted from other sources, particularly my wonderful friend and colleague, Kristina Brode. Psychosynthesis is a transpersonal model of therapy which was developed in the early 20th century by Roberto Assagiolo, an Italian psychiatrist who was a colleague of Freud and Jung. In his psychological model he included both the personal and spiritual aspects of the person. He sought to foster personal growth and self-awareness as part of the journey towards psychological healing and spiritual awakening. Put in another way, experiential transformation can give rise to insights that bring more self-awareness. This allows you to feel better about yourself and what you have to offer the world.

You will also need to be aware that as you listen to your Wise Woman, your intuition or your inner voice which doesn't want to be ignored or sidelined, your **inner critic** can start over-riding it. This is the part of you that is in dispute with your inner knowing and sees that it is its duty to keep you safe and under control. It is one of the most challenging inner obstacles for many of us to gain freedom from this self-sabotage. This inner critic can block us from having inner freedom. It may be there from the onset and can come in against your Wise Woman. Simply be prepared that this may happen.

One of the best methods to help you through your journey is to write your thoughts and feelings in a journal or a notebook of some sort. It is about you having the willingness to invest the required time in reflection and introspection. In psychosynthesis, your journal or workbook is seen as a tool for those sincerely interested in their psychological and spiritual development. It is private to you so you can be as free as you wish. Keep it in a safe place. It is your choice as to whether you share it with anyone else.

The journal can give you signposts on the path of your continuing growth. It can also give you the chance to go back over your day, or revisit an exercise and extract further meaning. Don't feel compelled to over-write – go lightly and enjoy.

Use your journal when reading this book, while doing the Visible Woman exercises or for reflection whenever you want. You can also include any comments from your Inner Critic. For myself when I have looked back at my old journals, I am surprised in a good way at what I've written. It helped me to see how strong my Inner Critic was. See what you experience.

CHAPTER 1

HEAR THE CALL
Be it a whisper or a shout

*'Inside every older person is a younger person
– wondering what the hell happened'*

CORA HARVEY ARMSTRONG

For many of us, life is not terrible and can feel reasonably okay; yet still we feel something is missing. For others, we have arrived at a place where things are definitely not right. We seem to have lost our way and we don't know what *is* right for us. We don't even know who we are any more. We are no longer celebrating our life but simply going through the motions. It's as though we are waiting for something to happen without knowing what it is. And as we 'wait' life can be passing us by.

Also, as discussed earlier, it seems that the effects of life's normal ageing process are some thing to be avoided at all costs. There is increasing pressure, on women particularly, to try and hold back time.

It's not just us ordinary folk either who feel we are rapidly becoming invisible in everyday life as we age. We've had the case of the BBC presenter, Miriam O'Reilly, being dropped from Countryfile because of her age. She also claimed that this treatment was sex discrimination as it is dished out to women not men.*

Another example is the lovely Australian model, Elle Macpherson, of whom a journalist wrote that she still looks terrific without make-up *but* there's no hiding those wrinkly hands. Never mind that she is a successful businesswoman who has also raised two boys as a single parent; all they focused on was her hands. Does anyone mention Gordon Ramsay's or Alan Sugar's wrinkles? No, of

26   * The tribunal upheld her claim that it was age discrimination but not sex discrimination.

course they don't. Men are nearly always judged on their abilities not their appearance.

No wonder so many women are considering just what life is all about. We are not only losing our visibility but we are no longer listening to ourselves. What is it you are waiting to happen before you'll start living fully? What is the Call for you? What will it take for you to change what isn't right in your life?

For many of us the Call is as subtle as feeling flat and stuck. Sometimes a New Year's resolution is enough to shake us out of it, but a lot of us feel unable to carry on and grind to a halt.

I say, don't let it go that far where you reach rock bottom or become ill take action as early as you can. When you first notice that things aren't right – those feelings nibbling at the edge of your mind – do something, don't let it over-run you.

You could take some of the following actions:

- Speak to a professional

- Speak to a trusted friend

- Get out for a walk in the park on your own

- Sit quietly and give yourself permission to let go of your feelings and thoughts

- Write or draw freely in your journal or notebook without holding back

- Sing, dance or just move your body to free up your mind in order to step back

My Call was more dramatic than most. So I heard the call LOUD AND CLEAR. It wasn't so much a call as a big shout! It was totally unexpected. I saw a Consultant one day, was hospitalised and operated on the next day for bowel cancer. After recovering, I realised that I'd let life slide.

For most of us the Call is a feeling that something isn't right. It might be that we slide into depression, or lose our job or simply lose our zest for life. For me, as I've said, it was dramatic, getting cancer and realising my own mortality made me see that I wasn't living the life I wanted or living it to the full. Life wasn't right but I was cruising along just letting things lie. Until I realised that I might not have a life left to live and I wanted to *really* live whatever life I had left and live it *my* way.

It was an enormous shock – not just for me but all concerned in my life. It is amazing what happens when one moment you think you are making the most of your life and then the next you realise you haven't been. I was made to wake-up and re-examine what I was doing. So that was my miracle – I was given my life back again.

Yes, my "Call of the Wise Woman" was quite unusual but not all are like that. It can come in as a little whisper, lots of whispers, a shout, a tap, loud knock and so on. It can happen through many painful causes, and we can also hear the message in inspirational music or books. It can happen unexpectedly through people or places we come in contact with. It can be a positive experience that makes you realise you've not been living life fully. You can fall in love and decide to rearrange your life.

Or it can be a sad experience. You may become overwhelmed by what seems like insurmountable difficulties, or just the ups and downs of everyday life. You can get thrown off track and become discouraged. You can feel like life has lost its edge somehow. This is when you need to take time out. Stop and listen to yourself to see what you are being told. The Call can come through health difficulties to make you stop to see what your body is telling you. Very few of us are in tune with ourselves so don't listen to any signals. I am saying that we can learn to be in tune with ourselves. We don't have to wait for something awful to happen.

When you choose to respond to your Call, it doesn't mean all will be well and you will be able to live life happily ever after.

No, not so and yet in recognising it, you are much more able to handle the ups and downs of life. My business card has on it: 'Life is what happens to you while you are busy making other plans' John Lennon. I'd already had a loud call when I was in my early 30s (I'll come back to that later on) so it seems once again I was not aligned with myself.

How did you react when you read 'Hear the Call'? What kind of reaction did it generate for you? Did you go into denial, gloss over or not even see the words? Have you heard the Call but chosen to deal with it another time? Do you know it's there but are avoiding doing anything about it? I'm going to ask you now to identify your Call.

Visible Woman Exercise

- Take a deep breath or two, be open and spontaneous and see if you can discover what *your Call* might be?

- If you are able to identify your Call, what might it be telling you?

- What would your usual responses be to hearing this request?

- I can't because……

- How did you feel when you saw your response(s)?

- Write in your journal.

As you get to know yourself and your habits or patterns much better, you will one day be able to take a step back and laugh internally at them. You will know yourself so much better and therefore not allow yourself to be taken in and be sabotaged by your inner critic.

Don't worry if you don't know what your Call is yet and are unable to complete the exercise, just be aware that you're working towards it. You will know by the end of the book.

You can revisit this exercise later and a good tip is to know that you can change your '*I can't*' to '*I won't*'" which gives you more of a choice. I *will not* means *you* have the power to do something about it. You are not a victim. Remember you do have a choice. You can also try 'Will I?' which can offer another possibility for choice.

With regard to my awareness of the difference; I've noticed that when I have said, 'I can't because I am too busy doing something which needs to be done' or, 'it is too much hassle to look up train timetables' for example, I have missed out on some interesting times and people. When I began saying to myself 'No, I won't do it', and stamped my foot like a child, I eventually ended up laughing and saying, 'Okay I will'. Try it for yourself and see what happens.

I'd like you now to get ready for your Visible Woman journey and here is my first full request for an exercise.

Visible Woman Exercise

Take a moment to choose your *typical* week and then write in what you do each week This is for you to see the reality of how you spend your time. Don't judge or censor it – this is for your eyes only. Remember the things *you* might not feel are important that you do daily or weekly, for example, sorting out the school activity requirements or phone calls you make. When you've finished, simply take some time to look at 'your typical week' and see how it feels for you. Ask yourself:

- What are you feeling as you see it?
- Were there any shocks or surprises – good or bad?
- Is there anything you need to change?

(If your journal isn't to hand, write these responses as soon you as you are able. You don't need any excuses for not doing it.)

Now tell me if there is anything you would like to change? If

	Monday	Tuesday	Wednesday	Thursday	Friday	Saturday	Sunday
Evening							
Afternoon							
Morning							

you're fine with what you see then that's great. If not, then I am going to be tough with you. Don't moan about being too busy and unable to stop. Simply acknowledge that this is what your life is like and you don't want to change it. No more messing around as this is what drains your energy. You can leave out the next part if you want to.

If there *is* something you'd like to change then please take another sheet. Do as before but this time visualise your *ideal* week with no holds barred, no judgements, reasons for why you couldn't, wouldn't or mustn't. Allow yourself to do it. Listen to yourself.

Take time to see how that feels and allow yourself to enjoy it. Nobody can stop you from allowing your ideal to be there – only you. You are the only one holding you back.

Now I'd like you to do the final part of this exercise on another sheet of paper.

This time allow in what you can't give up of your obligations but keep in what you also want from your ideal week.

Reflect on how this feels, how your body reacts when you do this. Ask yourself:

- What is it that you will need to do to bring about this more realistic yet more enjoyable week for you?

- What are the first steps you need to take?

- What support do you need to bring it about?

- Always make time for your reflections. Do this throughout the book

I had stopped listening to myself telling me that all wasn't right in my life. Even though I was juggling too many balls, I was coping wasn't I? I was doing what I wanted to do, or so I thought. Like many women, I demanded too much of myself and looked outside for validation. I tried too hard to meet my own and others' expectations. I ended up finding that I was leaving myself out of the picture.

Women are well known for their perfectionism. We try to

be all things to all people.   Let's hear from someone who knows she was juggling too many balls.

Carolina's story

'I am a happily married mother of four and I have done a lot with my life. I became a name and made a career in the advertising business. When I was 25 years old, I was Managing Director and a Partner. I became responsible for the creative team with 15 people involved. My agency was responsible for the launch of the new Swedish Bible translation. The campaign was such a success that one million bibles were sold out completely within five weeks and it was the Christmas gift of 1999.

'I was coping really well yet something was still missing for me. I decided to leave advertising. I went into publishing and produced award-winning books within the healthcare and food areas. I was still searching for something else when I got breast cancer.

'When I was well enough, I took the time to listen to my inner voice, and started up a new form of cancer rehabilitation. I opened a centre where women could be recommended to go to by their Doctors. As it was a charity, they could make a donation, if they could afford it, towards their treatment. I had made myself visible in this field with the programme I created myself. It was not easy as I had to deal with much red tape but I persisted and it has paid off. I am now running training groups for professionals who can use these extra skills to support others.

'I had needed that time out, to hear and see what my next step would be, and I have found my calling where I am being of service to the community.'

Carolina's story may have resonated with some of you. That sense of coping successfully and yet knowing there is something still missing but you don't stop and listen to yourself. Carolina stopped and heard her Call which meant change. And as you know, change of any kind can be exciting, difficult or frightening – or all of them. The fun kind you pursue and the others you tend to put off. Even when you're worried by a gut reaction to make a different choice or take a different path, you'll usually choose to ignore your inner voice. You'll do what seems easiest at the moment.

In my experience, change can be stressful although stress isn't always a negative factor. We can also become depressed by not being stretched enough. You can sink into lethargy and boredom which can cause problems for yourself and others in your life. I have seen this in myself and clients.

It doesn't always feel like it but you *do* have options and choices even if it's that you're indecisive or stuck. **The feeling of being stuck is simply that feeling you have when you want something different in your life.** The frustration and negative feelings around being stuck are often caused when you are not sure how to make the changes you want.

In my therapy room, I would often challenge clients to simply own their stuckness first and then ask them to say, 'If I wasn't stuck, I would …' and to see what came.

Visible Woman Exercise

- Why don't you try that yourself right now or whenever you feel stuck. Let go of your inner critic and respond spontaneously to:

- If I wasn't stuck I would

- Now list any responses from your inner critic

Learning both about how and what you are holding yourself back from may surprise you. You can take time out here to explore more in your journal or carry on.

You can also simply say to yourself, 'I don't believe you' whenever your inner critic tells you all the reasons you can't do things differently. Observe the bodily responses that occur. At least there will be some movement and not stuckness. One of my clients became really angry with me when my response was that I didn't believe her when she said she was not able to challenge the status quo in her relationship. She had moved out of her stuckness into the angry feelings which had been trapping her. She hadn't wanted to own her inner truth even if it was causing her problems.

You see, if you avoid 'unstuck', it could mean that you could live the life you're meant to live. It means you must bring about change in some way and as we discussed earlier, change can be scary. That's why our natural reaction is to want to retain the status quo even if we say and think we do want change. Your usual habits are preserving the life you normally have which means you're not ready to change. The latter is important for us to acknowledge. You can truly think you are ready and yet you don't move forward – obstacles happen and you give up. It's like being stuck in mud with the body going forward but the feet firmly not moving.

The decision to change can be painful and cause havoc around you. The **transition time** is when you're straddling two worlds – the old and the new – and it can be very uncomfortable, but that doesn't mean we shouldn't do it. We need to be willing to let go of our attachment to particular ways of doing things, rigid opinions, etc. What is required of us is to let go of ideas no longer viable, of beliefs and values that aren't ours, of people maybe. This last one was extremely painful for me as when I resigned from my organisation, my colleagues had been like a family for me but I felt that the values and changes being brought in did not fit with me.

This letting go of the old and becoming comfortable with the new may take months, even years. But standing in your own shoes is well worth it. You will avoid stagnation and learn to manage the process with less stress and more grace. This is a time to be willing to try something new, doing something different in your personal and professional life. Listening to your fears and doubts (and even others' voices and your own inner critic), deprives you of the opportunity to grow and develop. Remember we don't have to be stuck with our familiar fears and doubts. We can acknowledge them and then step back from them. Saying that, also remember that cautious discrimination is not indecision – it can be wise. We have checked, listened and on occasion decided not to go down that route.

When we do decide to change, the high that can come from 'jumping off the cliff' can also disappear. It's like having to relearn how to live. You could say 'girding your loins and getting on with it'. If you constantly think about everything that can go wrong, it's as though you are constantly on high alert. Imagine how it is when you feel or you notice particularly good feelings, take a moment to acknowledge it. This allows all the cells in your body to also feel good. It's like saving good feelings in the bank so you can withdraw them when you are feeling low.

Visible Woman Exercise

- List all the good feelings you have in your feel-good bank to draw upon e.g. laughter, pleasure, patience, etc.

- Choose one of them to use today

This can be the one you breathe slowly and deeply into today. Remember this action allows us to let in quietness and also to retain that calmness in our body cells. You can choose another of the good feelings for tomorrow, if you are feeling low or whenever you want to bring a smile within.

Here is Ann's story. She also kept telling herself she was fine and pushing away the voice that kept trying to get her attention:

Ann's story

'After leaving the business world to have my children, I thought I had found my niche. I chose to stay at home and look after it and my family. I loved cooking, entertaining, gardening and making my home look good. I was being creative.

'But over the years, those interests and all the other housekeeping wore me down. Something wasn't right and I didn't know what it was. And I was aware that I had allowed my family to take me for granted. One day I had had enough and I knew I had to speak with someone. I made time to do Irene's exercise on my typical week and what was important I allowed out my creativity. I chose flipchart-sized paper and coloured pens to represent different people and activities and I got a shock.

'Where was I in it? Where had I gone? There were many good times with my family, lots of fun and enjoyment, but I seemed to have disappeared over time. I no longer felt visible to myself or my family. I had given up on my possibilities and became this person I didn't know any more.

'It was time for action. I returned to learning. I got qualifications in reflexology, aromatherapy, holistic massage and reiki healing. Who knows where this will lead. I am still passionate about my gardening and photography too. When I get overwhelmed, I now take time out for myself and listen to my inner voice. I have a sense of myself as a person in my own right, my life back and the whole family, after some adjustment, is happier.'

Ann was now able to see that often it is not the situation that keeps you stuck but your *attitude* about your situation.

If we break old patterns of behaviour, we can open doors to allow a different way of life to emerge if that is what we want.

By having the courage to take on challenges small or large, as they arise, we have the opportunity to learn about ourselves and possibly discover hidden strengths and talents. We don't necessarily have to make a big splash in life, be famous or perform great public acts to have a positive influence on the world. There are many things that go on behind the scenes, quietly and unacknowledged. And sometimes just a smile and acknowledgement can make a difference to someone's life.

If we are not acknowledged, feel invisible or even dismissed for less than who we are, it is not a good experience – it can be very painful.

Visible Woman Exercise

- When you feel invisible, what happens in your body?

- What are you feeling?

- What are you thinking?

- How do you handle what is happening to you?.

- Now you have more awareness, what could you do differently the next time it happens?

Many of us can feel insecure and small inside when the person we're talking to looks over our shoulder to see who else they can be seen with. Even worse is when we're not even seen at all – when we are treated like we are invisible. This happens to many of us, especially as we get older. Other than perhaps in your profession, your views, opinions and even your voice can get overlooked or even dismissed.

When this happens to me, I acknowledge to myself that it is happening and then I choose to go with what seems appropriate at the time. I bring myself in, find my voice and make a comment. I may wear brightly coloured clothes on occasions so I won't be overlooked. And sometimes it really doesn't matter depending on the situation as I know I am present to myself.

But we also overlook ourselves; as we age we no longer really look at ourselves in the mirror. I know this for myself as I don't always recognise who is looking back at me. '*Who is that person I glimpse in the mirror? I think it can't be me'*.

The important question is when we actually stop and look in the mirror, do we like the person looking back at us? If your answer is 'No', then we need to ask ourselves why that is. If your answer is 'Yes', also ask yourself why that is.

Visible Woman Exercise

- I'd like you to stop reading right now, and find a mirror – any kind large or small. Then look in the eyes of the person staring back – YOU.

- What do you see in your eyes?

- How do you feel right now?

- If you could let her speak, what would your Wise Woman be saying to you?

- Take a few moments to write down your responses.

We normally don't like to look into our own eyes because we are frightened of what we'll see. Usually there are feelings of not liking what we see and we can become invisible to ourselves. You don't even acknowledge yourself – full stop.

It's fantastic if you can smile and enjoy looking at the 'you' facing you – good stuff – no judgements simply acknowledgement. There you are; here I am.

Over many years, I have run various self-development courses for women aged 30 upwards. When the course begins, I ask them to silently look around the room and see their reaction to the other participants. When the course ends, I ask them to look again at the others and notice if anything has changed. Their reaction is much more positive because they are no longer judging on a superficial level. They've had time to get to know one another on a deeper level – whatever age they are. They are no longer invisible!

We have to accept that we will have our ups and downs – that's life. And ageing is not all good that's for sure, what with wrinkles and gravity taking it's toll on the body not to mention health concerns. But it's not all bad either. There are compensations once we accept ourselves and the inevitability of getting older; the wisdom we build and that we can feel more comfortable in our own skin and feel less like we have to prove ourselves.

As we get older we tend to have a clearer sense of what is important and what is trivial. Others' opinions of us count less than how we feel about ourselves. We have much more choice on how we can dress and act. We can please ourselves. We can laugh and cry at ourselves and life much more easily. We can still enjoy ourselves, have fun and be daring.

Look at Dame Vera Lynn's life philosophy when she was 92: 'You can't do a lot about getting older but don't let it stop you from doing what you want to do.' What a woman!

With that wonderful philosophy ringing in our ears, let's end with the final exercise of this chapter.

Visible Woman Exercise

- What do you want to do with the rest of your life?

- Write everything down that you can think of even if it seems far-fetched or seems impossible.

Take time to reflect on your list and see if you are already taking steps towards any of these things. On your first glance it may not appear to be the case, or you can even be dismissive of any movement you are making. Or you may be pleasantly surprised to see that you are on your way. Sometimes that's because we unconsciously know what we want and what will be good for us. Therefore, record the steps you are taking that are aligned to what you really want, your heart's desire. Give yourself a pat on the back for unconsciously following your inner call. You've found out that you were on your path anyway.

Throughout the book be open and honest to hearing from your **Wise Woman** whether it be that of a whisper or a shout. If your inner critic voice comes in you have a choice of listening, telling it to go away or writing down what it says.

I'm not asking you to do anything with your answers right now. Seeing what you write down can make you confront your life then you have a choice to change it.

You have to shake yourself up once in a while whether you're stuck, feel invisible, feel confused or have that feeling that something just isn't right. Now is the time for **You** to be in charge rather than life doing it for you.

If Cora Harvey Armstrong's 'Inside every older person is a younger person – wondering what the hell happened' rings a bell for you, great. Then the feeling of being stuck is simply telling you that you need something different in your life. If you are not listening or hearing the Call to change it may be that you are not yet knowing or not wanting it enough. A useful exercise would be for you to allow yourself to visualise how life would be if you weren't stuck. Try it.

CHAPTER 2

YOUR WAKE-UP CALL
Stop pretending you don't hear it – wake-up now!

✳

'Life is just one damned thing after another'
ELBERT H. HUBBARD

I have shared Portia Nelson's poem below with my clients as it echoes the message behind recognising our Wake-up Calls. It is a lighter way to introduce the subject of having the choice to do something different in our lives.

Autobiography in Five Short Chapters by Portia Nelson, American Renaissance Woman.

> **I**
> I walk down the street..
> There is a deep hole in the sidewalk.
> I fall in.
> I am lost … I am helpless.
> It isn't my fault.
> It takes forever to find a way out.
> **II**
> I walk down the same street.
> There is a deep hole in the sidewalk.
> I pretend I don't see it.
> I fall in again.
> I can't believe I am in the same place.
> But it isn't my fault.
> It still takes a long time to get out.

III
I walk down the same street.
There is a deep hole in the sidewalk.
I see it is there.
I still fall in ... it's a habit.
My eyes are open. I know where I am.
It is my fault. I get out immediately.
IV
I walk down the same street.
There is a deep hole in the sidewalk.
I walk around it.
V
I walk down another street.

In other words, what Portia Nelson is saying is that if you always do what you have always done, you receive what you have always got. Does that sound familiar to you? As I said, it does to me and to so many of my clients and friends. We just keep on hanging on in there doing the same old thing (however much we feel we are doing it differently), until one day we wake-up. We start to see that we aren't victim but have the power to do things differently. Let's do an exercise which will bring awareness of your own entrenched habits to the fore.

Visible Woman Exercise

- What is it you do repeatedly?
- What results do you get?
- What has caused this pattern?
- Are you willing to see other ways of doing things?
- If so, when will you do something different?
- I'd like you to make your answer into an affirmation – I will do …..when….…..

If you are unable to see any other possibilities for now then simply acknowledge to yourself that this is what you are doing – and that you need to revisit this again.

I can offer some possibilities too. Remember before, during or after you do something you can ask yourself. 'Is this what I want to do?' You can stop reading this book, get up and move, do something different then try out saying 'No' or 'Yes'. Or to answer yourself, you can try saying, 'I'm not frightened to jump' in order to take the needle off the habitual response – even if it is only for a moment. You can visualise yourself and applaud your changes as you are building this movement internally.

My Wake-up Call of almost dying from cancer caused me to listen to what my Wise Woman was saying – stop being superwoman! I was trying to juggle too many balls. I wasn't listening to myself. I only heard it when I was actually back in the land of the living. I was being told not only that miracles do happen but that it was time that I reconnected with myself again. It was time to take stock of where I'd come from, where I was going and what my next step would be. It was now a matter of who and what I wanted to keep or let go of in my life.

This wasn't an easy time for me. I had to reassess my life; to re-look at people and activities, and to see who or what uplifted rather than drained my energy. I hadn't realised what a good prop I was for some people and now I needed to prop myself up.

I've been blessed with a wry, Glaswegian sense of humour. I grew up in Glasgow and as the saying goes, 'You can take the girl out of Glasgow but not Glasgow out of the girl.' This has shaped and formed my outlook on life. It can be wonderful to laugh at the craziness of life and I mostly do so, but I can assure you that I was not laughing then!

The realisation that I won't live forever, I mean really facing it, meant I was able to reflect on what I had done with my life. I was actually surprised by how much and how many adventures I had experienced. I'd visited more places than I could have dreamt of when I was young. I was also aware of what I had not yet done. I chose to let this go for the time being and to instead simply acknowledge the gratitude that I was still alive, and that I'd lived a life.

Allowing oneself the time to be grateful – appreciating all the good things, big and small, that have happened in our lives - has been known to boost the immune system. For me it worked.

This was something I badly needed. At that point, I took life easy and stayed with the healing process. Getting back to good health, and feeling confident enough to think about driving my car on my own, took some time.

Just as I needed space to heal, so you will you. This book isn't about having quick-fix answers. *It'll take time and it is up to you and what you choose to take onboard.*

You are the expert on your life. I can only share with you my professional and personal experience of what can work and what I know doesn't work. I'm not perfect, no one is, in fact, striving for perfection can cause us problems. I still make lots of mistakes!

As I've aged, I've become more realistic about both my personal limitations and that many of life's difficulties are outside of my control. I am only in control of my attitude towards the things I can't change. I have become less willing to keep trying to prove how good I am. Yet on the other hand, I have become more aware of what I have to offer. This is what I call maturity and it offers a new richness to my personality and it can do the same for you.

So no matter your age, it's not too late to decide to wake-up and make the most of the rest of your life. Every day you will get wake-up calls, even if you pretend you don't hear them. All day long you are faced with making choices (tidy up before going out or not, phone and deal with mundane or pressing issues, address a problem we have with a friend) some are easy and some more difficult. People give many different reasons for not being able to be something or achieve certain things such as, I am not clever enough, I don't have enough money, I'm too young or too old, I want to stay invisible…. These are all limitations which can and will stop you from being or doing what you would like. The lack of belief that it might actually be possible or be achievable, is what's blocking you.

Let's look now at what is limiting or blocking you whether it's the internal (yours) or external voices (others), as well as the reality of your life.

Visible Woman Exercise

- What would be on your personal limitations checklist e.g. I am too frightened to move outside my comfort zone?

- Are you able to change any of your beliefs about yourself?

- If there is one thing you can begin to do today, what is it?

Don't judge yourself harshly if this one is difficult. Your inner critic has too much freedom in your life. Be gentler on yourself.

Having looked at your limitations, you now want to be able to look back on things you can be proud of as these more satisfying memories can actually help you in your life and career.

Visible Woman Exercise

- List all the memories that make you feel good inside

- Give yourself time to really savour them again.

- Choose one of them to draw upon as you go about your day.

Don't forget that memories are malleable. They change as the years go by and sometimes alter, taking their character from the way you are feeling in the present. So when you're depressed, you will more likely make a sad selection from your memory bank. It can seem as though you've no happy ones. The past is not a fixed and unchanging thing and, even though you can't alter past events, you can alter your perspective regarding them.

Of all your memories, it is those events that cause humiliation that are the most indestructible. That shame may be buried but it is always there somewhere and the humiliation can cause us to hide our vulnerability. If we numb our vulnerability, that shame, then we will numb our birthplace of joy and creativity – our lust for life. We need to embrace our vulnerability – include it wholeheartedly as it is part of us. Only then will this part of us begin to grow. We won't have to be ashamed of ourselves and can begin to stand tall, allow ourselves to be seen and know that we are enough in our uniqueness. We are worthy!

Visible Woman Exercise

- First, ask yourself if you're willing to look at any horrible feelings you may have from your past. If you are, write down a memory that usually you would rather keep buried e.g. when you so wanted to be accepted and yet were laughed at and excluded instead, or being told you were a nuisance.

- Is there another?

- How might it or they be leaking out into your life right now? Some memories may be more strident or very timid in their dealings with others – see what yours is.

- Then sit quietly and ask your Wise Woman for some help or comfort after this workout. You may find that holding a cushion close to you, stroking a soft toy or imagining having your hair stroked can also offer that feeling that someone is on your side. Remember that your Wise Woman is always there waiting. She appreciates you regardless of what you do or say.

The point of all this is that it is time to begin to appreciate yourself. Do you? I know for myself and with clients and groups, appreciation can be so hard. Like many people, I was brought up to believe that it was big-headed and I'd get 'too big for my boots' if I praised myself. I was also told that I'd soon get put in my place for it by the world. So let's challenge these old beliefs and do the following:

Visible Woman Exercise

- Make a list of all that you appreciate about yourself
- Take this time to enjoy these qualities. Let them in.
- Which one are you choosing today to enjoy?
- I wish you enjoyment with your choice.

A suggestion I have is that you schedule one appreciation a day for the next week or keep them in your diary so that you can take them out when you need that boost. I put one at a time on a card on a shelf in my workroom. When I see it, I get a smile inside.

Belated appreciation
– better late than never!

For me, now that everything is spreading wider or moving south, I don't always recognise the ageing woman in the mirror. I cannot believe it when I look at photos of my younger self and know that I didn't appreciate myself back then for how good I looked. I am only now appreciating myself for all I have been through and I still enjoy my lovely smile.

What about you? How do you feel when you look at the younger you? Are there tears? Do you smile as you look or are you angry at the loss of vitality or innocence? Are you pleased that the younger you has you on her side now? Whatever you feel, simply acknowledge that emotion is your truth today.

In my work as a psychologist, a wonderful thing I do with clients is to ask them to bring and look at photos of themselves at different younger stages in life. It can be so revealing and even painful for some. Like Ann in the last chapter, most ask, 'Where did she go? What happened to me?' I have a photograph of me at three years old gazing straight out past the camera at the world and it still touches me even now. What life in her. That young me is saying '"I'm here and ready for something new'. We never really lose how that three-year-old felt. It just gets buried under life as it happens. But you can still access that younger you.

Visible Woman Exercise

- Please look at photos of yourself when you were young. Choose one that appeals to you – perhaps you find yourself saying, 'Where did she go?'

- You may smile, laugh or cry as you see her again.

- Stay with her for a little while then be open to listening to what it is she is saying to you. Allow her voice to be heard.

- Breathe in her message (write it in your journal).

- Finally, how will you choose to honour her voice?

When you have made your decision and are ready for something new, allow it in. Life then seems to take over. People or events come into your life and help to move you on your way – give you direction. I know for me, the more lightly, and yet seriously, I take myself (listening to my Wise Woman), events and people fall into place. Life paradoxically becomes more fun. This has happened often to me. And I have so many wonderful people to be grateful to – and some don't even know how they helped me.

The Wake-up Call of mid-life is when you can finally start to realise you are a person in your own right. As the philosopher, Dr Carlo Strenger, said, 'If you make fruitful use of what you've discovered about yourself in the first half of your life, the second half can be the most fulfilling. Most can anticipate a second life, if not a second career.' I would definitely agree with that. Don't ever say again, 'Oh, I'm too old or it's too late for me.' It really is never too late. Or to put it another way, if you know you could be living a fuller life why would you let life just slip away half-lived?

I mentioned earlier that I'd had a loud Call in my early 30s before cancer in my 50s. This was when I was querying, 'Surely there has to be more to life than this? What's life all about?' and so on. This was also a time of struggle and strain for me. It was only when I was approached by someone (while I was standing on a street corner doing market research) that life slowly began to make more sense. This was the woman who helped to change my life – my Scottish friend Anne. That weekend she'd started a discussion group and she invited me to come along. I did and my life took off as I began my psychosynthesis training and became so open to learning. I had come home to myself. I was in my own shoes and not those imposed by others.

This is also the time for you to 'come home to yourself'. It's time to do what you are here to do and always wanted to do. Remember we are all interesting in our own way. There is only one of you – you are unique. And, even if it takes a while to realise it, you all have a story to tell.

Visible Woman Exercise

- What is the story you would like tell to the world about?

- If your life was a fairy tale, what would it be?

- How is it being acted out in your life?

Now that you have this awareness, see if this information enables you to understand your life so far and any changes you may wish to bring about.

Difference creates opportunities

Some of us hold ourselves back by wishing we could have someone else's talents. How do you feel when others stand out – jealous? When you are confident in your own abilities, you feel far less threatened by others' abilities. In fact, their talents can inspire you and you can celebrate them. You are meant to be different, and you need to learn to embrace your unique qualities. I firmly believe that **difference creates opportunities**. To know that you have stories and ideas which are not only interesting and unique to you, but can also connect and inspire others, can give a feeling of contentment inside.

Remember this and accept you can't be good at everything. Okay it would be great if we could be but where would be the challenge in life? Others can do some things better than you – maybe even a lot of things. Not being good at everything simply confirms that you are human, welcome; that's life – accept it. Knowing your weaknesses doesn't mean you have to dwell on them or broadcast your failings.

The challenge is to apply yourself to what you like and to what comes naturally. Focus on what you're passionate about or you will just be mediocre. Or, as Steve Jobs of Apple says, 'Your time is limited, so don't waste it living someone else's life – don't let the noise of others' opinions drown out your own inner voice.' Great advice!

Remember, the whole point of answering your Call, of me

asking you to do so in this book, is that if you disregard your inner voice, that calling, your road becomes more and more difficult. You are safer following your own road. Even better than that, it's more rewarding; it's yours, and only yours. But to do what you really want, sometimes you have to overcome great obstacles. And you can still have bad days. Life doesn't become perfect and effortless. Let's see what enables us to follow our own road.

Visible Woman Exercise

- List the ways you do nurture yourself when you have bad days

- What support can you call upon, if needed?

Once you know where your support may come from, the big question you will ask yourself next is, 'Where do I start?' First you have to look inside and ask:

The Visible Woman

- What makes me truly happy?

- What qualities do I want to embody?

- What gives me the most passion?

- Or, as is said in psychosynthesis training, what makes my heart sing?

- Take time to reflect on this exercise and see what good or surprising answers you find.

If this is difficult or you draw a blank, you could ask again in another way:

Visible Woman Exercise

- What am I good at?

- What qualities do I want to embody?

- Am I discounting any of skills that I take for granted?

- What would my close friends or colleagues say about me?

- How can my qualities, skills, life experience be used towards what I want?

- What's the dearest and most creative possibility for me?

- What's most meaningful and important for me?

See if by doing this exercise you're able to start to visualise the next step for you on your personal journey. A very simple way to do this might be to ask yourself, 'what would be the title of a book about me?'

The above exercises are to help you learn to honour yourself in whatever form it takes and to consider how you contribute to the larger community. Look at what you are doing at present, for instance, you are not simply your job. Say you are a hairdresser, you are not simply a hairdresser but someone who is creative and helping others' self-esteem. How often has a person come out of the hairdressers with a new 'do' and felt like they could conquer the world? That feeling is worth a million pounds. So go over your list and breathe in what you *do* offer the world. Don't forget the little things you accomplish each day.

Visible Woman Exercise

- Look over your day – what have you accomplished today?

- What are those tasks you discount or take for granted?

If you're having trouble recalling your triumphs, you're not alone. Over the years, most participants in my groups have difficulty remembering the good ones. You'll probably recall in detail all the times you've failed or made mistakes. The brain remembers events more easily when they're accompanied by strong emotions. If you're only able to summon up your failures, you won't be ready to take the risks that can lead you to your future successes.

You might be like Margaret who remembers that she could share only a few things she appreciated about herself during one of my group sessions.

Margaret's story

'It was much easier for me to tell the others all the areas I was no good in. When I was reminded, I realised that I had forgotten to share that I had got myself literally off the floor. I had faced up to the fact that I was an alcoholic (even after 35 years of being dry) and had taken the steps to re-integrate myself back into society. It had taken me a lot of courage and a lot of support from my family and friends.

'It was quite a journey. I had to face up to the damage I had done to my family and myself with my drinking. After much soul-searching, I applied myself, retrained and became a counsellor. It was my low self-esteem which was my downfall, as to the outside world, I was an attractive, together, competent and very able woman with an envious lifestyle. At times, I wanted to scream out, 'If you only knew,' but of course I never did that. I now know that this is called the "imposter syndrome" and somewhere inside I was always waiting to be found out.'

Margaret understood that this imposter syndrome can affect women in any profession or any walk of life. This self-sabotage seems to come from when are young. You need to remember though that feeling incompetent and actually being it are two different things entirely. You are as smart as others think you are but *you* must believe it.

Learn to accept that self-acknowledgement is *not* a form of conceit. Face and banish that old belief and rejoice in your successes. Then, I want you to build your self-esteem by recalling *all* the ways you have been successful. Your brain will then be filled with images of you making your achievements happen over and over. The more you acknowledge these, the more confident you become in taking on, and successfully accomplishing, new ones.

Visible Woman Exercise

Take some time to remember when you were a child and try to respond to the following questions:

● What were you told you were good at whether inside or outside the home environment?

● What do you remember doing easily and effortlessly?

Now recall other occasions in your life when you were admired for these things.

● If you feel you no longer have that skill or quality, where has it gone?

● How did you let it disappear?

Now, thinking of yourself in the present, answer the following:

● What are you being told you are good at now?

● What do you find easy now?

Can you see how we allow ourselves to become invisible and lose our passion when we don't value what comes naturally to us? Just because these qualities come easily and we can overlook them, doesn't mean they're not priceless. What you may take for granted, others will find difficult. You don't always see and appreciate not only what you are good at but all that you are actually doing. This could be because you feel unworthy and you discount others' praise or appreciation of you. Does the phrase 'Oh, it was nothing!' sound familiar? Stop and gratefully say 'thank you' instead.

The Juggler in Action

Visible Woman Exercise

- Stop to think of all the balls you are juggling in your life.

- What are they?

- How are you managing?

You might be really surprised at your juggling skills. It's time to give yourself a pat on the back. It doesn't matter if you occasionally drop one or two; what's important is to see just what you are juggling and how amazing that is.

I remember many years ago, a business colleague and friend couldn't believe how I was managing the household budget with so little money coming in. She praised me for my skills, which was a surprise to me as I was busy punishing myself for my lack. Hearing her different perspective gave me great encouragement and helped to change my view of myself. This is what I want for you. I can tell you now: you are amazing. Acknowledge this and you will be even more amazing.

On many occasions over the years, I've been confused as to why I'm being praised for something that felt easy for me. But there will always be times when you doubt a particular task or skill you can ever master. For me it was learning to drive. Although I did pass first time, it took me some time to agree with my driving instructor that I was ready for my test because I was so scared of taking it. The tightening of the stomach, the sweaty palms, the increasing inability to focus, the tingling in the arms and hands, and the anxiety about doing it correct or having the right answer – sound familiar? You all know about fear. It's part of the human condition.

I am now aware that my fear was a sign that I was learning and growing. It wasn't a sign that I wasn't good enough or not ready. It lets you know you are doing something new and that you have some learning and preparation to do. The fear of speaking in public has never gone away. The knowledge that I can do it has encouraged me to take on the challenge whenever I'm asked. This time I include my nervousness. I take deep breaths, include my feelings and thoughts, and then remember this is not about me, it's for the audience.

If you accept you'll always be learning new things, doubting your ability will always be a necessary step in the process. It's a sign of growth. For me, passing my driving test was my ticket to freedom – to be more in charge of my life.

The only way to beat your fears is to do whatever you are fearful of. To trust that whatever happens to you, you will be able to learn from it.

Visible Woman Exercise

- What is it you are frightened of right now?
- How is that stopping you from living your life more fully?
- Is there any help or support you are needing right now?
- Who could help you with this?

Let's now look at another view of fear – others towards us.

Visible Woman Exercise

- Who would feel diminished by your intelligence, creativity, go-getting, knowledge, or other strength, skill or talent you have?

● Are there ways in which you hide your abilities, talents and stay in the background to prevent a jealous reaction?

● What happens to the dreams and ideas you supress because they may challenge those closest to you?

What I've described above is sometimes called **The Tall Poppy syndrome** where if you stand out or put your head above the parapet, you can be shot down. We've seen it in the media when those of merit are resented, attacked or cut down. So no wonder you're frightened of taking the risk and being a success. Therefore, you may be cautious for good reason. Then again, when you were younger you may have witnessed someone having taken a risk and been hurt or shamed, or worse, this may have happened to you. This caused you to become afraid of living your life fully. For me, I can still remember being forced to perform at family parties and being ridiculed when I said no. That was one of the times I decided not to stand out or give them what they wanted. Yet it still had consequences, manifesting in my fear of public speaking as an adult.

You've probably heard of the following quotation, frequently wrongly attributed to Nelson Mandela, but actually from *A Return to Love* by Marianne Williamson. I'm repeating it here because I find it beautifully sums up what I've been explaining to you:
'Our deepest fear is not that we are inadequate. It is that we are powerful beyond measure. It is our light, not our darkness, that most frightens us. We ask ourselves, "Who am I to be brilliant, gorgeous, talented, fabulous?" Actually, who are you not to be? You are a child of the universe. Your playing small doesn't serve the world. There's nothing enlightened about shrinking so that other people won't feel insecure around you. We are all meant to shine,

as children do. We were born to make manifest the glory of the universe that is within us. It's not just in some of us; it's in everyone. And as we let our own light shine, we unconsciously give other people permission to do the same. As we're liberated from our own fear, our presence automatically liberates others.'

Someone who was not afraid to let her light shine and whose call to change came more than once is Jane:

Jane's story

'I had always been outgoing, a not afraid of the spotlight type of child. I soon learned that this confidence was not so accepted by others and they tried to put me down. Even when young, I realised that I felt I was on my own and became lonely when this happened and only had my father's support.

'To a certain extent, I fitted in with what society wanted me to be. I had dampened down myself and began to lose some of my lively confidence. It was when a friend of mine died unexpectedly in her 30s that caused me to take stock of my life, to see where I had come from and where I was now. I did not know where I was going. I also realised that I had made myself invisible through not allowing my talents to shine. I listened to myself and decided to expand my personal training practice.

'I heard another Call after my father died. He had always been my big supporter in whatever I choose to do. Again painful loss was behind my re-looking at my personal and professional life. I am now writing children's books as well as articles on Alzheimer's disease. Where this outlet will take me, I have no idea except that I know I am on the right track again. I now truly have the opportunity to realise my dreams. From this place, everything is falling into place. I am again listening to myself, feel in tune with my life and am standing out and being seen.'

Visible Woman Exercise

Let's look at the fear of being a success in another way:

- What did you decide when you were young?

- How did this decision hold you back?

- How is it still holding you back?

- What are the ways you can move forward so as not to be held back?

One of the ways to loosen the grip of the decision holding you back, is to look in the mirror and tell yourself that you are not that age any more. You now have YOU on your side and it is your time. See how that feels. Smile as you pass the mirror each time – it doesn't matter why or if others think you are daft – go ahead, trust yourself. This worked for me and everyone I've suggested it to.

The price you pay is high when you keep yourself small and you're being dishonest to yourself by not letting us see more of you. Playing small doesn't serve you. This is how *you* make yourself invisible. Yes, others may ignore you and you could just blame them but you are colluding with them.

I really want for you to be the best person you can be for yourself. The world will then follow as you show them your uniqueness. You don't have to actually do anything. By being less self-conscious, it takes the spotlight off you and onto those you want to motivate to live up to their potential.

Visible Woman Exercise

- Once again, take the time to be still and then identify the feelings that are holding you back from life's next adventure.

- What is it keeping you from the life you really want, and know deep down you can have?

- What are the steps you can take to deal with this? List them one at a time.

Remember you don't have to take these steps alone. There are support systems available that you can ask for help from, for example, family, friends, coaches, therapists.

What you are working towards here is having a more positive attitude. The trick to a positive mind is to focus on what's going right for you and appreciate what you do have. But as we are only human, this isn't always possible. In the worst of times, it can be just too difficult. I believe that we all need to take time out to be with our feelings.

Our feelings need to be acknowledged before we can move on. I don't advocate the eternal Pollyanna view of smiling and being happy about everything. Accepting yourself as you are will reduce stress and anxiety by the simple, although not always easy, act of loving yourself. I am using acceptance here in the context of surrendering to the reality of your life – not resignation (victim) or rebellion (distorted power) – so that you are no longer in denial about it. It can then be useful to see your glass half full instead of half empty, i.e. your attitude towards yourself and your life.

As I've said earlier, most of us are prejudiced in some way, and judge people before getting to know them. We make conclusions about their character, intelligence, abilities, trustworthiness. So try to be open to seeing others as being worthy of your respect, however difficult it may be.

We frequently judge what we fear we do ourselves. Perhaps you have heard others say – they are just show-offs, not very intelligent, don't fit in, etc. Let's try this exercise for more clarity on ourselves.

Visible Woman Exercise

- What are your judgements of others normally about?

- Where do you think these came from?

- Do you think you could possibly have similar parts in you? This can bring awareness of how you view yourself.

We've all been conditioned to some extent by family, teachers, media, and society at large, which can either be helpful or detrimental. However, you've arrived where you are today so you need to take responsibility for your own attitudes and beliefs, no matter where they came from.

Are you willing to look at things in a new way? Some call this **reframing** i.e. taking a new look at something which is familiar to us, finding new perspectives, discovering new dimensions or exploring new meanings and interpretations.

Visible Woman Exercise

- What new perspectives are you willing to explore?

- Are you willing to try this out in your daily life?

- When, if you are?

- Or, why, if you're not?

- I trust you will gain awareness from seeing things differently, looking at the bigger picture, and seeing other possibilities.

At times, we can be overwhelmed with issues internally or externally. The following words of Roberto Assagioli may be of use to you:

'We are dominated by everything with which our self becomes identified. We can dominate, direct and utilise everything from which we disidentify ourselves…'

The process of stepping back and looking for the bigger picture is called **disidentification** in psychosynthesis, which means that you do not need to become your problems, conflicts, feelings or thoughts. Disidentification can lead to a sense of 'I *have* the problem rather than I *am* the problem', which can bring a sense of relief for many. When I first went into therapy, this was such an amazing realisation for me. I felt so much lighter and freer. It can help you in the same way.

Even when life feels tough, you can still feel that you are making a valuable contribution to it. And when you are ready, try to view life in the longer term by seeing the bigger picture. The Call of your **Wise Woman** is always there. Whatever you are being asked to do, can make a difference to those who come after you. It is your legacy for your imprint on the world.

The final Visible Woman exercise of this chapter is a visualisation. Visualisation is a way of awakening your intuition, creativity and your imagination. So allow yourself to relax and let go of all you have been reading so far.

Visible Woman Exercise

- I'd like you to take a few deep breaths, close your eyes and focus your attention inwards. Simply be open to whatever comes up for you during this exercise. You don't have to worry or give up if this is something unusual for you to do. Simply give yourself permission to be as present as you can.

- I'd like you to imagine you have gone into a magical shop where you feel comfortable and at home. Take some time having a look around and then I'd like you to see a photocopier.

- I'm now going to invite you to open and place your hand on the photocopier and take a copy of your hand.

- When you take out the photocopy, on it will be an imprint of your hand.

- This imprint will tell you what your legacy is to the world. The response you get may be in words or pictures.

- Again be open to the unexpected as it may not make immediate sense or have a connection with anything you are immediately aware of.

- What is your mark or imprint on the world?

- What does it mean for you?

Don't worry if you are puzzled or confused by your picture, symbol or words. Simply accept and trust what you are given. Allow it to be within you and then write in your journal. More clarity can come when you don't try too hard to understand.

Enjoy being *You* - there's no one else like you. You are a fantastic woman. Your Wake-up Call is here, ready to be taken. You can be visible to the world because you are visible to yourself. You don't have to depend on the outside environment's response all of the time. You can trust yourself.

Sometimes life can be just one damned thing after another. This is also the dawning that your life *can* be different when you wake-up and make the most of the rest of your life. It is not too late. It's time to stand up and be counted. Look in the mirror and really see yourself with all your faults, talents and qualities and simply acknowledge that you love this woman – this woman who is you.

CHAPTER 3
....

WHAT DOES THE CALL SAY?
Be open to a world of possibilities

'Every time I close the door on reality, it comes in through the windows'
JENNIFER UNLIMITED

What my Call was saying took a different form from my previous one. That earlier one was all action, exploring and training; learning more skills and learning about myself. It led to me eventually becoming one of the 'been there, done that, got the T-shirt' women. This time around, my inner Wise Woman was saying take life easier. Listen to yourself. Life can manage fine until you are ready to join us again.

I just wanted to be. However, there was still something nagging me, although I didn't know what. Perhaps like some of you, I felt I was getting on a bit to be starting a new adventure. My excuse was that I didn't want to deplete my energy. This was actually true. I was exhausted just showering and dressing. My passion was 'out the window and long gone'. Now I am asking *you* to think again. You may be too old to be that ballerina but you can still dance, take lessons or simply enjoy attending the ballet itself.

No, don't make excuses; I can already hear them starting to arise in you at this point. I've heard my own and others' excuses, and after fighting changes I feared, I've found if you accept change gracefully and be a lifelong learner in whatever form then you can gain the most out of life. There *is* a world of possibilities out there. It is about being open to them that enables us to stay young at heart. Practise seeing the glass half full and be eager to see what tomorrow brings. No matter what your age, never stop pursuing your dreams, however they manifest themselves now.

In my work, I've been amazed at how many give up on their dreams and then wonder why they don't feel good about themselves or are even 'unwell'. A lovely woman, Patricia, who was my client had always wanted to run a clothes shop, particularly after the children had left home, but somehow couldn't do it. She didn't get support from anyone in the family or from herself. She resigned herself to fitting in with everyone else. No wonder life became grey and miserable. She was simply going through the motions. You must know others who seem half alive or not present enough in their own life. Their passion or lust for life appears to have all but disappeared.

The breakthrough discovery in our work together was the extent to which she put off things no matter what. Procrastination is a habit that makes a hefty contribution to this half alive state. Do you recognise what I am talking about? It's that thing most of us do when we have something to do that we're afraid of; we will do anything other than that task. An example might be dealing with those we think have some sort of authority over us when we speak with them on the phone or in person. We find other things more pressing and somehow we just have to do those first. I find myself cleaning, washing windows, anything except getting on with whatever it is that really needs doing. What we're doing when we do this is **diversion**. It is usually because we've not yet got the courage to face life's reality.

So let's hear all of your reasons for not doing anything about your habit of procrastinating. Simply list them in your journal. By now, you know it's better to let your thoughts out onto paper than pretend they are not there.

One way to tackle what you really need to do is to *feel the fear and do it anyway*; take a few deep breaths and then get stuck in before you over-think it. Clearly look at any issue that you are not facing and see the ways you *can* make that phone call or do that task.

I suggest you now do another exercise which will help you to be clearer on facing your fears.

Visible Woman Exercise

● List all the reasons you are still stuck and not moving on.

● What is it you are really afraid of in moving towards what you really want?

● Once you've identified exactly what it is, list say 3 steps (or even 1 step) you are going to take to alleviate your fear.

If you think you are unable to take this step, then I suggest you allow yourself to see the worst and best possibilities of acknowledging and facing your fear. There is always a deeper reason behind us being stuck so don't be too hard on yourself. Just allow yourself to be open to rummaging inside to find out what it is.

Also remember to examine your motivation as the same action can be either positive or negative depending on your reasons for doing it. An American friend of mine, Nan, always used to say that 'a good deed never goes unpunished!' She meant that we needed to check what our motivation was first. So ask yourself:

Visible Woman Exercise

● What am I motivated by?

● When you think you've finished with your answers, wait and allow in anything else that comes to you.

● You may be surprised at your responses.

Get your deeper motivation out and on the table – be honest – only you will know the truth. It is better for you to acknowledge this consciously rather than denying it. Once you know what it is, it will be a relief whether your motivation is for fame, gain, to benefit others, to keep yourself busy or just to have fun. When you have the awareness, you can then truly choose what you want to do, and how you want to be.

When you find you're dreading or avoiding change stop and have a think; you may be cheating yourself out of new and wonderful opportunities. 'Ignorance is bliss' is a saying that could apply to the Anne I mentioned earlier in the book, who read a book and started up a self-help group. Nobody had told her that you were 'supposed' to have a degree, experience, or other qualifications to do this. She did it and it was a success. She set up the group without fear. Anne helped many people and went on to train as a psychotherapist. She now has her own training establishment.

Visible Woman Exercise

- What have you done in your life in blissful ignorance?

- How did it turn out – good or bad?

- What did you learn from it?

- Sometimes when you think a part of your life was a waste of time, if you think again and make a list, you can be surprised at how useful or constructive it might have been.

Isn't it good to look back and laugh, cry or shake your head at the crazy things you've done? You, as an actor in this game called life, can shape your future by working with or against energy forces to create it the way you want it to be.

Remember nothing ever stays the same. The nature of life is change. You can stay stranded on the familiar and known when over on the other side is the unknown which can be frightening. In psychosynthesis, which is a **transpersonal** (more than a personal) model of therapy, it is said that *the known can be a prison with golden chains that bind you to it.*

The Co-founder of Maggie's Cancer Caring Centres, Maggie Keswick Jencks, is someone who didn't stay stranded but pushed the boundaries of the cards life dealt her to bring about change for those following her. Here is her background:

As well as being multi-talented, Maggie had vitality and determination in abundance. She needed every ounce of these when she was told she had just a few months to live in 1993. After gaining a reprieve for 18 months by joining a trial for metastasised breast cancer, she put all her recovered energy into fighting for the supportive adjunct to medical treatment which she felt was desperately needed by anybody having to learn how to rebuild a life with cancer as part of it.

She persuaded her medical team at Edinburgh's Western General Hospital that they needed partners who could help their patients with stress reducing strategies, psychological support and the opportunity to meet up and share with others in a relaxed atmosphere.

As the inspiration for Maggie's Cancer Caring Centres, which are found in many parts of Great Britain, Maggie proved the importance of an imaginative, inspiring place for people to turn to at such a critical moment in their lives, somewhere which feels joyous, a beacon of hope.

Maggie has certainly inspired me and many others. This woman, in the midst of everything going on for her personally, stood up and stood out and made herself visible. That's why I am donating ten per cent of my book sales to this charity as well as doing my sponsored walking each year in aid of Maggie's Charity. I have done their 20 and 10 mile London Night Hikes. My son, Ian, has also supported the charity through taking part in a duathlon and raising sponsorship money.

Most of us have met, at some time in our lives this kind of person. Someone who enthuses and inspires you. You feel alive and ready for anything as their passion rubs onto you.

Visible Woman Exercise

- Who are the people, whether living or dead, that have inspired you?

- What was it in particular about them that touched you?

- If you value certain qualities, where are those qualities being expressed in your life today?

- If they are not expressed in your life, then you are starting the process now by recalling them.

- How and where are you expressing them, or how and where could you express them?

This magic power of enthusiasm is within all of us. It is the fuel that gets things done. It's the contagious energy that inspires us.

'Whatever you can do, or dream you can, begin it. Boldness has genius, power and magic in it' Goethe

The road to spontaneity and bravery is often the road to excitement and fulfilment, to life's adventures. You're saying *yes* to life.

Haven't you found that after you've done something you were afraid of, you wonder what all the fuss was about? It wasn't as bad as you thought it'd be. And when someone asks how it turned out, you've almost forgotten what it was you were so frightened of. Take some time to reflect on such occasions. These were the 'Yes' signposts on the road of your life. They are calling to you again. Stop and listen. I would suggest that you can also draw those signposts from your birth to now on a piece of paper or in your journal. Again you may be surprised at what you discover.

Visible Woman Exercise

● Make sure you have time to do this and then allow yourself to think about your life's journey. Just imagine you are seeing it on the TV and you can stop, pause, and restart it whenever you want. Allow yourself to be open to the signposts on the way and make a mark on the paper which symbolically represents a turning point or crossroads which you took or didn't even notice at the time. Do this from birth, through teenage years, right up to present day. You may then wish to write more fully about the signposts for your own learning and discovery.

When I've wanted people to reflect on their life, another method I've used is to ask them if they are living the life they want to be living. I consider this is a good question to be asked by us all at the end of each year or at birthdays. These are the obvious markers in our life. Remember how you looked at your ideal week in the first chapter, now I am making the task bigger. Write down your ideal life and see what are the little steps or what 'seize the moment' jumps you can take.

Visible Woman Exercise

● What would your ideal life look or feel like?

● What are the steps you can take towards making your ideal life a reality?

● What 'seize the moment' jump can you make right now?

Maybe you can allow yourself to think of something you would like to do that *you* feel is beyond your skills, intelligence, age or gender. First feel the fear. Then start planning how you might accomplish what you want to do. You also need to let go of your inner critic perhaps by asking yourself the following: **how would I feel about someone who criticises me as much as I criticise myself?**

Visible Woman Exercise

- What is it that is not possible or achievable for you?

- Why is it not possible?

- What if it were possible, how would your life be?

Take some time to explore this possibility as specifically as you can. Where would you be? What would you be wearing, seeing, feeling, thinking and doing? Is there anyone else with you? If it is aligned with your Wise Woman's Call, then that's the pull towards your next step.

If you're willing to look fear in the face, you'll be able to do much more than you ever imagined. I never thought I could write a book but it was there somewhere inside me just waiting to come out. I simply needed to own that inner voice and be open to who and what was happening in my life. If you've something you dream of doing, don't sell yourself short, you may need a helping hand, like me, but get the help you need and just go for it.

Learn to trust your own inner voice, your call and your values when making decisions and determining what's right for you. If doubts emerge, as they will, really choose to stay true to your inner compass and feel free to adjust your course if necessary.

That old saying 'if at first you don't succeed, try and try again' is so true. You have tried and will have learned from your attempts. It is simply information on how your insights can strengthen your future efforts. In Roberto Assagioli's *The Act of Will,* a good description of the 'call' is given by Carl Jung. He says that to have a vocation means in the original sense 'to be addressed by a voice' and that is your Wise Woman calling you. I wonder what the call says to you. Mine simply says, 'You <u>can</u> do it – whatever it is you want, go for it.'

Life has a way of pulling the rug out from under you, for example, when you lose a job, face divorce or become ill. Life isn't easy – problems arise on a daily basis. Success in one area can run alongside defeat in another. The antidote to the reality of life is to not allow the voice of discouragement to overcome you. You can't prevent uncertainty, as that is how life is, but you can learn how to handle it better.

Accept you don't know what's going to happen next. Don't drain your energy in denial or resisting reality. You can learn to relax in the face of the unknown as much as you are able to. It is not easy, let's be honest. It is amazing though when unexpected things happen and you feel vibrant and alive. Those good-time feelings are the ones you put into the feel-good bank to draw out when you need to.

Visible Woman Exercise

- What good-time feelings do you have in the bank that you can draw upon?

- Make a list of them and allow yourself to choose one and savour it.

- Really take time to enjoy it. Bring it fully to life again. Make a commitment to yourself to breathe in one each day.

Talking about commitment, here's a question for you to ponder on. Why do so many New Year's resolutions fail? Probably I'd say because deep down you didn't really commit to them. Why is it difficult to make commitments? Again, the fear of having to change, being fully responsible for your life, closing the door on other options. You know the one – if I do *that* I might miss out on *this*.

Visible Woman Exercise

- Why do you avoid the commitment to change?

- Make a list of all your reasons.

- What might the pay-off be not to change?

- Does your answer surprise you?

As American business philosopher Jim Rohn said, 'If you really want to do something, you'll find a way. If you don't, you'll find an excuse'.

It's normal for you to worry about things, find excuses – you are only human. The following exercise will be helpful for you to do. With each question answer as honestly as you can and you'll gain insight into how to better handle life's situations. You can also take the exercise in stages.

Visible Woman Exercise

- Is there an event that is coming up or is in the near future, which you are worried about?

- What are the things you are worried will go wrong?

- What would it look like if it went wrong?

- What solution can you come up with for each thing that could go wrong?

- What are you willing to do to get the results you want?

- How can you motivate yourself?

- How can you take pleasure in doing what needs to be done

to get the results you want?

● What can you do today to get things moving in the right direction?

In my therapy and coaching work when I have a client with a problem or worry, I invite them to visualise someone they admire – even if it's only from seeing them on TV or reading about them – and then to imagine that they are them. I suggest visualising themselves standing in this person's shoes and looking at their problem or worry. I'd like you to try this visualisation now.

Visible Woman Exercise

● Close your eyes, allow yourself to be still and then visualise the person you admire and imagine you are standing in their shoes.

● How would this person handle the problem or worry you have?

● What would they tell you?

● What are you willing to do about your worry now?

● Take time to think this through.

● When you have finished, you can write about your experience in your journal.

Remember you can always invite your Wise Woman in to support you. She is always available to consult and inspire you. She is totally there for you. She knows all your fears, doubts, joys and qualities. She doesn't judge you and looks at you with total, unconditional love. Are you willing to act on the insights you receive? You may find no solution comes straight away and your communication may not be in words. Be open to it coming in an unexpected way, for example, as a sentence that stands out when you are reading or you may hear a song that gives you a clue or a book on your shelf could suddenly catch your eye. It may also appear as a sudden, intuitive knowing.

Being flexible in your mind and spirit is equally as important as being physically fit. We all need to be open to the unexpected. You may know of someone who, for whatever reason, is slower in their body but excitedly open to learning and new happenings. Remember you can always discriminate to check out any answers you receive.

Being willing to make that 'seize the moment' step - exciting, scary and very hard to do – you'll grow new wings to meet the challenges as you move forward in your new venture regardless of what it is. Remember that you'll have all your past life experience, intelligence and your Wise Woman to draw upon.

Most of us are too busy to stop and listen to our inner voice. Our passion for life is waning. We don't even know why we pointlessly rush around sometimes. Here's another exercise which causes you to look deeper.

Visible Woman Exercise

- If you feel caught up in the frenetic pace of life, ask yourself:

- Is my rushing positive or negative?

- Am I you running towards well-thought out goals?

- Or am I running away from the loneliness of fear and failure?

- Simply acknowledge your truths. You don't have to do anything else.

Most of us have those times when life's pace just feels like a huge weight on our shoulders, or we give ourselves a headache by having too much on our mind. Let's move on to an exercise that has been useful for me and others in shifting this pressure.

Visible Woman Exercise

- Make a list of at least 20 'musts', from practical 'to do' lists to qualities you want, for example, I must be a good mother or a good gardener or I must always be calm and contented or a good organiser.

- Get them out of your head and onto paper - see the pressure you put on yourself.

- Read each one aloud and be aware of the effects or changes in your body as you hear them.

- Then let go and relax.

- Now change your 'musts' to 'I could'.

- Again, read each one aloud. Take note of what you feel happening in your body.

- These 'musts' are what stop us from our 'lust' – our passion for life.

In psychosynthesis, we normally do this exercise in a group and it is very powerful to hear all your musts repeated back to you. Try it with a trusted friend.

This is a good technique to enable you to move from pressure to choice. It's also a great way to get an awareness of what you do to your body, as you can damage it unknowingly. This can manifest through headaches, stomach pains, shoulder ache, tiredness, changes in blood pressure and even more serious illnesses. Again, this is also a way we reduce our passion as it is more 'must' and less 'lust'.

When we see what we do to ourselves, you can understand

why many of us want someone to come and fix our life. That fairy godmother with the magic wand – *yes please*. Sorry, it rarely happens. If you don't help yourself first nothing will happen. It has to start with you. Remember you have to get off the potty!

If you feel like you're stuck in a rut, or on the potty too long and need to make a change then the first thing you need to do is to try something new.

Visible Woman Exercise

● What can you do today that is new for you?

● What can you do to help yourself, small or big?

● Try it out.

By making the effort on your own behalf and by reaching out, you will get responses to your efforts. Again quietly close your eyes and take some deep breaths, offer any issue up to your Wise Woman. This will help bring about an answer. It may be because you have simply stopped and got off the treadmill of worry that you are able to find the answer. You've allowed yourself some space to focus again. That's when the answer comes.

Something I've learned is that the mind can only hold one thought at any one time. In my work I use a technique called **opposition thinking**. When an undesirable thought occupies the focal point of your mind, immediately replace it with an uplifting one. It's as if your mind is a giant slide projector with every thought being a slide. Whenever a negative slide comes up on the screen, you act quickly to replace it with a positive one.

This has enabled clients to have a respite from their imagination.

It is said that discontentment arises when reality is no match for imagination. Pictures affect your self-image. Your self-image affects the way you feel, act and achieve. It is reported that Einstein said, 'Imagination is more important than knowledge'. Use creative envisioning to see yourself as you want to be. Allow yourself the freedom to fly with this one. The following exercise is an example of how to do it.

Visible Woman Exercise

- Close your eyes, take several deep breaths, relax and visualise pictures of all you want to be, to have, and to attain in your life. Write down what you see in your journal.

- Choose your favourite image.

- Mentally rehearse the way this will unfold.

- Have a clear vision of your outcome.

- Then create positive pressure by breathing the picture inside you to keep you inspired.

- You may also like to draw what you're imagination has shown you.

If your inner critic comes in with all her or his usual thoughts or words, simply thank them for being a good ally and protecting you in your life, or simply tell them to go away – you're not listening.

A tip I have learned is never set a goal without attaching a timeline to it – a precise deadline. Put the date in your journal. There's no reason why you can't adjust the date! Research has shown though that you need to perform any new activity like the visualisation technique for 21 days in a row, i.e. the time it takes to create a new neural pathway.

Change does produce uncertainty about the future and brings up a wide range of feelings, particularly as you move into the next half of life. Ask yourself:

Visible Woman Exercise

- Where am I now?

- What do I want to do with the rest of my life?

- What are the thoughts and feelings that come in when I hear the above?

- What choice will I make now?

A question to ask yourself to help you make choices is, 'who would you be drawn to – someone who is middle-aged and miserable or a confident and mature woman still growing and learning?' You can allow yourself to not only be open to this but also to be flexible and unpredictable in your life.

Honor Blackman, an actress, said, 'I nearly always take a dare. If it's something I haven't tried before and it's within the realms of common sense. I might fall on my face, but where's the shame in that?' Words from the wise and she is certainly not allowing herself to become invisible, nor being too worried about what others think of her.

Change is part of our destiny. The changes we make need not be big and dramatic. Remember you can make changes in manageable steps. It is one way that you can have control.

Visible Woman Exercise

- List all the unexpected changes that have happened in your life.

- How did you handle them?

- What would you do differently now if you were faced with them again?

- It is important to know that you have this ability and are learning.

Your internal change precedes the external change. 'This is how I am and will always be' gives place to 'nothing is carved in stone'. It is said that the only certainties are change and death, and we resist both. The urge to grow is often uncomfortable so we collude to prevent it and to maintain the status quo. But growth requires change. Inertia also seduces us to maintain the status quo. Change is hard work! Feelings of inadequacy and failure can be stimulated by the experience of our immense potential.

Some of my clients have said that they were going through the motions but not really living. Life seemed flat, grey, dead even if it was full of activity, people and events. Energy just ran out. There was a feeling of emptiness, a vacuum, a sense of waiting; nothing seemed to be happening. These can be short, low periods – times when you feel below par. Though it may have the feeling of depression, it may simply be that you are not listening to yourself. If it is treated too readily as medical, say with anti-depressants, you may be extinguishing away whatever is seeking to come in – perhaps the Call of the Wise Woman. The Call doesn't go away, it will find a way to come back even if you don't listen now.

Visible Woman Exercise

- What was happening to you when you had times, when life was flat and dead?

- How did this greyness manifest in your body, feelings and mind?

- What was your view of the world?

- Who or what enabled you to come back into life?

Those occurrences of what can seem like withdrawal to the outside world, may actually be essential. During my cancer treatment, it was seen as peculiar that I wanted to be on my own, in my own hospital room with the TV and the lights turned off except when needed. My withdrawal was necessary to my recovery. Sometimes withdrawal or a period of quiet reflection can be signalling a transition between two distinct phases and can preclude change. For the new to come in, the old has to fall away. The recognition that life is out of balance and the intention to make different choices is the first step in change.

In my work, I have observed that many middle-aged clients enter therapy or coaching to deal with **stagnation** rather than crisis. Although issues around ageing and finitude are also present. Highly stressed or depressed people turn their attention inward on themselves, losing interest in or becoming out of touch with what's going on in the world. My objective is to bring the best out of people by raising their awareness of what they are doing to themselves. Helping them to know when it's good to withdraw and when it's not, which can take some time to learn. It's also vital to help them to rekindle their passion and to realise it isn't completely dead but has just gone underground for a while. We fan the embers together.

Finding your true passion and doing what's important for you doesn't mean destroying yourself or others in the process. Your passion feeds you but if it distorts with compulsivity then it can destroy you. I have had clients who have ridden roughshod over others because they were so driven and haven't taken anyone else into account.

The Visible Woman

- How can you include your passion and others in your life?
- Picture yourself being in the world with this passion. How is life different?

- How are you dressed, talking, walking?
- What are you doing?
- What are the steps you can make today?
- Go on, I dare you; try a step out.

You could consider the possibility of taking a step. But remember, when you are thinking negative thoughts, your mind filters out everything positive. This vicious circle needs to be interrupted. Just like a TV programme you don't like, turn down the volume or change the channel. Even if you manage this only for a moment, you are still breaking the habitual thinking pattern. Try it now!

You also need to be aware of the effect your body language has on you. When your body language becomes like a depressed person's – slumped and focusing down to the ground use the technique of **reverse feedback**. Stand up like a confident person, put your shoulders back, hold your head up high and move with a positive sense of purpose. Smile and nod as you would with genuine enthusiasm, and Act positive to feel positive; 'Act as if', which is an old psychosynthesis technique. Roberto Assagioli saw this as a powerful tool for change. 'This technique consists in *acting as if* one actually possessed the desired inner state….. Thus we can, to a large extent, act, behave and really *be in practice as we would be* if we possessed the qualities and enjoyed the positive mental states which we would like to have. But this is not all. More importantly, the use of this technique *will actually change our emotional state.*' You are being told here that your mind and imagination are powerful tools for change. Therefore, whatever it is you need to have or be in your life right now, take a risk and act as if you already have it.

When we sing, for example, it is very good for us. It releases endorphins, the chemicals which have a positive effect on our mood, and it also improves our breathing and posture. It can boost confidence too. I know I feel better within myself when I sing along to music on the radio.

Another technique I use with clients, who need to have a break from their anxiety, is called **paradoxical intervention**. This is whereby you do the very thing you've been trying *not* to do. For example, a client might have difficulty leaving the house as they need to keep checking whether the door is locked. Their anxiety level becomes very high. I encourage them to deliberately check it time after time. 100 times, if necessary, until they get sick of it and angrily stop, or even laugh at themselves. Another example might be when someone lies in bed worrying. I tell them to deliberately stay awake or get up and do the housework that needs doing. The brain begins to get the message that the negative habit which has been bullying is unwelcome.

Visible Woman Exercise

- Make a list of all your continual worries

- What do you habitually do?

- Now try the paradoxical intervention technique, and do whatever it is you don't want to do any more.

- What happens?

I admire the writings of William Bloom and his research on endorphins. In his book "*The Endorphin Effect*", he calls that subtle but all-pervading awareness that regardless of what's going on around you all is well, 'the Smile Within'. It shows as a state of relaxed alertness with good feelings in your body and positive thoughts. I can achieve this by thinking of my grandchildren when they are playing. That brings a smile inside and to my face.

These feel good hormones can get triggered when you recall all your good times.

Visible Woman Exercise
Make a list of all your good memories. Pick one and describe:

● What was happening?

● Who was there?

● What were you doing?

● What were you feeling, hearing, sensing?

● As you recall this memory, squeeze your thumb and index finger five times. Then whenever you do this, those feelings will come back. You've created an endorphin switch. Every time you'll find it easier to relax and enjoy the memory.

As I have said earlier, acknowledging your reality enables you to have the choice of whether to do something about it. Once you commit to change you will find that your fear will lessen and your hope and energy will increase. Again you can only stay stuck for so long when even that gets boring.

Something you need to be aware of, and fully experience, is your ambivalence and resistance before you can bring about change. Ambivalence is a basic fact of life. Life isn't black or white, good or bad. I learned in psychosynthesis that it is '*both-and* not '*either-or*'.

We can forget that life is indeed very scary at times and being alive is a special kind of bravery. Your life is not set in stone. It's a continuous process evolving and developing. You have options and choices all along the way. Yes, you've been influenced by your past but you do have the ability to alter your present and your future. As you accept who you are, you have the choice of becoming more visible, more unique, of being open to all the possibilities out there.

That is the paradox of life and of living.

Come to the edge of your comfort zone – go on I dare you to take that next step. If that means taking time out, then that is your next step – so do it. Remember also that there is a big wide world out there just waiting for you – get ready to fly. One, two, three, go!

CHAPTER 4
....

IT'S YOUR CALL

Stay on the sidelines or be inspired
and take action.

*'I try to take one day at a time, but sometimes several days
attack me at once'*

JENNIFER UNLIMITED

At some point when I was in intensive care, it did seem that I was on the sidelines. It was all happening around me. I had no choice. I was totally dependent on the hospital staff's care. I was unable to move in my paralysed body. My husband and son were the only ones allowed at my bedside. My future daughter-in-law was allowed in once I had stabilised and was not on death's door.

So it would seem I had to stay on the sidelines or be inspired and take action. More bluntly – the choice was life or death. Somehow or at some time I must have chosen life.

Following this crisis, in many areas I was much more confident – in facing death what else is there to fear – but in others I became more anxious. There was no rhyme or reason to it. I think I just became more natural in my responses and reactions – more myself.

I chose, therefore, to focus on building up my immune system when I eventually left the hospital. I sought out many forms of help – healing, acupuncture, homeopathy, reflexology, massage, kinesiology, and taking supplements.

Gradually, I tried many different forms of exercise. I am now focusing on my keep-fit class, pilates and walking. I did the Race for Life with my daughter-in-law and my six year old granddaughter in 2010. Little Lydia was wonderful in how she just kept going. We intend to do it again every year.

This led me to completing a 20 mile night hike around London (utterly exhausting mind you) in aid of Maggie's Cancer Caring Centres, which I mentioned earlier. I didn't believe I had the stamina to finish but with a little help from some wonderful women (thanks especially to Kaz), my body showed me I could do it.

Visible Woman Exercise

- What are you doing to support your immune system?

- What are the lessons you've learned about how you lower your immune system?

- How do you remind yourself to support your immune system?

- How do you encourage/motivate yourself?

One thing that supports me, apart from physical exercise and care of myself, is that I have always known that it's important to wear clothes that express you. And to see what they say to the world. As women, we're social animals and want to fit in, be attractive and be seen as successful and visible – even if it's been society that's conditioned this. As actress, Dame Helen Mirren, said, 'The best thing about my age and stage (in life) is not having to bother too much about things. I bother about how I look but although I bother I don't really care.' What she means is she makes the effort to look good but she doesn't worry about the world's response after that. What a wonderful attitude to follow. You now have the freedom to choose the clothes that fit your personality and feel good on you – being comfortable in your own skin.

Although I do want to point out that, as Helen Mirren describes in the same passage, '…. your own skin becomes slightly uncomfortable because you look at it and say, "What happened to my lovely skin – where's it gone?". This is a reality that happens to us all unless we get cosmetic surgery done or exercise 24/7. I am not sure what the answer is except that it is important to accept the fact of who we are and what we look like. I guess it is up to each of us to do what is right for us.

Remember, even with wrinkles you can still look good and have the time of your life by dressing with a bit of a flair and standing out. And if your boobs touch the floor, go to somewhere like Rigby and Peller and get fitted properly! You don't have to be mutton dressed as lamb but can still look stylish and modern. This is another way for us to stay visible. We can easily sideline ourselves by thinking it no longer matters what we wear or how we look.

It's not about going out and spending lots of money for a whole new wardrobe. It's about spending time finding out what your style is. Try putting what you already own together in a different way. There are stylists who can help here and maybe an honest friend could be just as useful.

Have a think about your clothes; the dominant shape, colour and style.

Visible Woman Exercise

- What are your clothes are saying about you?

- Are they congruent with what you want to say about yourself?

- If not, how can you do it differently?

Talking about clothes, here is Sue's story. She definitely did not sit on the sidelines after she took the time to listen to herself.

Sue's story

'I was 46 and had just married for the second time (widowed at 28). After having done a variety of financially rewarding jobs, I was earning a substantial income as an Account Manager and travelling all over the UK. My usual sunny disposition disappeared entirely as I hated that my role was changing. I was constantly stressed and had turned into someone who couldn't get out of bed and kept bursting into tears. My sense of failure was colossal. Even my husband was at his wits end and didn't know how to deal with me.

'I spoke with a friend about how life was "lacking". She asked me to think about what I was good at. At that time I was so low I couldn't think of anything at all. However, after brainstorming, we came up with all the things I am good at and would love to do. Within an hour, I'd chosen my new career, handed my notice in and signed up for the training with a provider I adore. Impulsive, mad, yes but I have never looked back. I also changed my exercise routine and introduced calming and relaxing yoga into it.

'I am now an Image Coach and within 12 months of making that choice, I was promoted as a style expert on TV; offered a publishing book deal (four books in print); launched a website; and featured in national and local magazines and newspapers. I delivered specialist workshops for women with breast cancer and provided educational and inspiring sessions for personal and corporate clients. I became the first image professional to become fully qualified on both sides of the Atlantic.

'My work concentrates on how women can live a fabulous life. So despite the fear, I did it anyway. I love my new life and every day is exciting'.

Sue realised how stressed she was and brought yoga into her life. As we age, stress can take a toll on our bodies and minds.

Excessive stress is not good for our health as the symptoms of stress can be so wide ranging. It pushes up blood sugar levels, raises blood pressure and the antibodies that fight off infections begin to drop. Colds and flu are an example of what can happen. You need, therefore, to reduce your stress and increase your resilience. Your resilience is the key that enables you to pick yourself up when life offers up one of its unexpected offerings. A quick, stress-busting tip is to STOP – even for just a moment – breathe deeply and then ask yourself, 'is this life or death?'

Meditation has been approved for use in the NHS. The two main effects are on the mind – calmness and clarity. It gradually allows you to still your mind. You then understand what is really causing you stress and, therefore, become more self-aware. I used to think I had to literally stop thinking but it's not so. You simply acknowledge what you are thinking, all the thoughts that crowd in, accept them and allow yourself to be with them.

In order to try and counteract the effects of stress, you can explore what works for you as an individual. Some of you might choose walking, reading, meditation, joining a gym or running club, cycling, pilates, listening to music for relaxation or dancing to it for exercise, or whatever you feel like at different times.

Visible Woman Exercise

- What do you do to reduce your stress and increase your resilience?

- What have you done today or this week?

- What could you build into your life for just ten minutes per day?

Time Out

You know what I love? Walking along the seafront at Westcliff-on-Sea, eating a Rossi's ice cream. I then sit on a bench just looking out to sea. The simplicity of this also represents my passion for life. There has to be a park, a lovely café or an area of natural beauty near you where you can do something similar. You may have to rearrange your time but see it as looking after yourself rather than leaving it for, 'when the time is right'.

Doing something similar, could be seen as the positive aspect of sitting on the sidelines. You are relaxed, watching the world go by and have the freedom to allow your mind to wander. This can allow you to be more positive in seeing how you are coping with the stresses in your life. You must know what it's like to be around someone who exudes a positive life force compared to someone who is stressed. You are only human so you worry. What you worry about is unique to you but you can tone it down. It not only takes its toll on your health but undermines all your activities.

Visible Woman Exercise

- List three of your worries right now?

- What can you do that might help?

- Are you willing to put that into action?

- If yes, when?

- If no, why not?

Minor worries can get put into perspective when you take those moments of 'time out'. Many of us have had tough times in the past. It's how we deal with it in the present that counts. There's a saying used nowadays that makes me smile: 'get over yourself' - sometimes you need to allow that one in.

Don't forget to laugh because when you laugh you lower

your blood pressure, reduce stress and increase oxygen levels in your blood making you more energised. Endorphin levels are increased and even your muscles get a workout. If you're feeling down and want to laugh, you have to make an effort by thinking about, watching or doing something that makes you laugh. It works for me to think of my grandchildren when they're running around playing. It really brings a smile to my face. For me, I think there is nothing better than having a real belly laugh with others when we are sharing jokes or being silly. I really enjoy my 'fat club' (exercise class) friends as we laugh with one another and come out of the class feeling much better all round. A friend of mine cuts out, or prints funny sayings or jokes that make her laugh and brings them out when she needs them.

Visible Woman Exercise

- What is it you do to make yourself laugh or what can put a smile on you face?

- Choose that or a memory and allow it in right now

- Simply be with it.

While you're letting that in and allowing that memory to settle inside, let's return to the subject of ageing again. Like it or not getting older is inevitable – time marches on and waits for no one however much we try. Some day you're going to have wrinkles – if not now, then at some time in the future whatever you do. Though, as I've said before, you can still look the best you can by taking care of your hair, makeup and clothes for your own sake.

Hear the wise words from the actress, Shirley Ann Field, 'I'm not in mourning for my looks. I don't think you need to be, you just have to take a bit more care. Women should keep themselves in good shape. It's a question of not becoming overweight, but also not being too aware of age; not allowing yourself to be. I would never let myself fall apart, so long as I have good health. A nip and tuck is fine, if it makes you feel good, but it's important not to end up overdone. Being older, you have to be better groomed but wear less make-up than you used to.'

Remember too that when the inevitable happens and your youth begins to fade, keep your heart young. There's a saying by Satchel Paige: 'How old would you be if you didn't know how old you was?' I think this applies to most of us, inside we don't feel the age that the mirror is reflecting back.

Visible Woman Exercise

- How old do you feel inside?

- How old are you in reality?

- Are you able to live with this contrast?

My friend, Marta is an attractive, creative, jewellery maker. She has such flare with her outfits and her work. Here's her story:

Marta's story

'I have had to cope with family problems while at the same time going through a painful divorce. For a long while afterwards, I felt I had aged greatly. I didn't laugh any more. I could not be bothered in how I dressed or how I looked. I even had no interest in how I wore my hair which had always been my pride and joy. I did not even notice that this was happening to me. The making of jewellery, which was my passion no longer inspired me.

'When I look back, it is so painful to see the difference in me. I had become so dowdy and old for my age. I had let myself go and had made myself invisible. One evening when I was having dinner with Irene, I saw her take a deep breath and go quiet. She then asked me why I was choosing to be and act older than I was. I did not take offence. I knew she was right. I had allowed my fire

to be put out – I had lost my sparkle. I had not taken up my call. I cried and cried and knew that I had allowed my despondency to take me over. It had got in the way of living.

'*Now I can say that my sparkle has come back, my passion for life and I am able to acknowledge that I am part of life again. I am off to Italy to do a course and to enjoy myself, learning, meeting people and the long, warm evenings drinking wine. I am once more visible to myself and the world*'.

Good on Marta, she is back home with herself. As you get older, one way we can lose our sparkle or passion is by focussing on our aches and pains much more. If you can do something about them, then do it. If not, try to be cheerful by contacting your good memory bank, that smile within. This is also when your support system comes in handy as you can scream and shout (let off steam), and have a real moan about the ageing process. Then you can laugh together, which allows you to come back to a much lighter view of life again. My family, old friends and colleagues are my support system. I've made such a long journey over the years with the latter.

Visible Woman Exercise

- Who or what is your support system?

- When do you remember to use them?

- There's no excuse not to keep in touch with emails, texting, Skype and the phone. Remember though, there's no substitute for a live meeting.

If you've neglected your support system, as it grows again you begin to realise that holding back your exuberance, your passion, makes you old before your time. Keeping an open, questioning and curious mind makes life more interesting.

Visible Woman Exercise

- When was the last time you made a new friend?
- What helps you to be, or to make life more interesting?
- How often do you allow that in?

Most of us start out with the intention of being happy but creating that intention may cause some resistance from our inner critic or those around us. We are so used to being in our comfort zone that we can subtly stop ourselves being happy. Let's explore why that might be.

Visible Woman Exercise

- Are you used to struggling or suffering?
- Is that part of your identity?
- If so, what would you name this part?
- What does it want from you?
- What does it need from you?
- What is the gift it has to offer you?

In psychosynthesis, we call these parts of us **sub-personalities**. When you name them, you are including them so you can get to know them, and not be frightened of them. For example, you could say you have parts you've called your struggler or sufferer. These sub-personalities normally come in when you are young. They protected and enabled you to survive and handle life. Unfortunately, these parts stay around too long, like loyal soldiers always on guard to keep us safe.

When you recognise and accept your sub-personalities, you can allow them to be integrated. This usually comes about by seeing what it is they want from you, then what it is they really need. When this need is fulfilled, they have a gift for us from the energy released in them. Some clients have found it helpful to draw their sub-personalities and get to know them that way.

Parts can be in opposition to one another, for example, your 'inspired to take action' part and your 'stay on the sidelines' part. If you're identified with any one sub-personality, you experience that you *are only* that sub-personality. This sub-personality's attitude is all that's available. The behaviour is compulsive, the views are narrow-minded and the feelings are limited. You need access to your entire personality if you're to be able to choose alternative or appropriate behaviours. An example I can offer is that when a client's children went to university, she was bereft as she had been so identified with her 'mother' sub-personality that she couldn't see that life had any meaning except through that part of her. She found herself making larger quantities of food, baking more cakes than needed for herself and her husband. It took her a long while to reconnect with herself and the rest of her personality.

Visible Woman Exercise

- List some of the sub-personalities you have

- Who are the most familiar ones?

- Who is the main one?

- What is its view of the world?

- Has it outstayed its welcome?

- What is its gift to you?

As women, we're often fond of, and really proud of, our ability to multi-task. This definitely comes in handy, but for your sanity you need to make boundaries – say *no* to doing too many things at once and to being over-scheduled.

Visible Woman Exercise

- How do you make time for you without interruption or multi-tasking?

- What are the arrangements that clamour for your time and attention?

- How can you find creative (clever) ways to say *no* to your family, colleagues, phone, housework?

Saying *no* doesn't mean that you suddenly stop responding to the people you care about, or start shirking your responsibilities. It means that you are not being increasingly driven by them. You can stop for ten minutes and simply breathe deeply and relax before the family come in. You can make time on your way home to 'be' (relax) before stepping through the door.

I can already hear you saying, 'I feel guilty about not doing ......' Did you know that guilt undermines your self-esteem? We are only human, jobs will always need doing, so don't let unfinished tasks drag you down. You use up so much energy pushing them away. Your energy is your life force. If you don't take care of yourself, you'll reduce your vitality and won't be at your best for yourself or anyone else.

Visible Woman Exercise

- Make a list of uncompleted tasks.

- How do you feel when you see them?

- Choose one task that you can easily complete and do it now.

- See how you feel as you tick off that task from your list.

Hopefully you will learn to feel less guilty and stressed.

Modern life is necessarily stressful to some extent. Every day we face a multitude of pollutants and chemicals in the air, and in our food and water. In addition, we may have demanding stressful jobs that involve long hours of travelling, running homes, bringing up children, and usually trying to fit in hectic social lives, too. Because time is short we invariably cut corners. We eat convenience or junk food, we don't get enough sleep or exercise, and we often smoke or drink too much as a quick-fix to relax.

Nutritionist, Patrick Holford describes how the body treats all toxins as a matter of urgency and works on processing them to render them harmless, or 'detoxed'. The body's focus on 'cleaning up' leaves less energy for everyday processes of cleansing, healing and renewal. Over time, the body can't keep up the pace, the strain shows on the overworked liver and kidneys and the body's performance slows down. The effects of this come in many forms: continual fatigue, infections, skin eruptions, headaches, digestive problems and even serious conditions such as ulcers, cancer and heart disease.

It is well known that physical exertion of at least 20 minutes stimulates production of endorphins. It is responsible for what is known as the 'runner's high'. Remember though that you don't have to run or go to the gym. This endorphin release can also be achieved by walking briskly to work or say dancing. So when you want to lift your mood and nothing else works, move your body. Then, after a while, when pleasurable feelings start, focus on these enjoyable sensations. This allows them to sink into your body and circulate more fully.

I'd invite you to be creative now and allow yourself to sit quietly, gently breathe. Then be open to trusting your inner wisdom and simply ask:

Visible Woman Exercise

- What are the different ways I can make life more pleasurable for myself?

- Make a list.

- Are you willing to put an appointment in your diary to do one of them this week?

- Again you may be surprised at your answers. It can be good to write them in your journal.

I know that when I feel good, my family and others also receive the benefit of my enjoyment in life. All the above helps to build a general psychological confidence as people who make life more pleasurable become used to feeling good inside. They also feel more able to be visible in the world and therefore get noticed and acknowledged more.

So the important lesson for you to learn here is to develop more self and body awareness. However, while it's important to take care of yourself, it's equally important to stop taking yourself so seriously. A major cause of negative thinking and poor health is self-absorption. This is ironic as we need to do this to get to know ourselves better. If we see it in the positive sense then the main issue is to raise awareness. The more awareness you have, the quicker you can catch yourself before you dive into old negative thinking or patterns of behaviour. With awareness comes choice and in psychosynthesis, choice is what it is all about.

When I was doing my first degree, during the experimental psychology module I remember I could not understand when a lecturer gave the classic example of how if you put a frog in water and let the water slowly heat up, the frog will do nothing. It will not jump out of the pot but slowly boils to death. However, if you put a frog in hot water, it would immediately jump out. Back then I could not see what this was a metaphor for. Now I can. We slowly allow ourselves to sink down in the slow morass of life as we don't notice it because it is a gradual process.

So many of us put up with things until we have no energy left to do anything about it and we become invisible not just to the world, but to ourselves. Many convince themselves that this 'prison' is totally fine – nothing wrong with being boiled alive! They think they have no choice. It's now time to wake-up.

Visible Woman Exercise

- What has caused you to sit on the sidelines and put up with whatever it is you are putting up with?

- What steps are you taking to get out of the slow morass of life?

- Remember you have a choice once you are conscious of what you are doing.

Sometimes we can sit in our 'prison' with all the lovely possibilities and do absolutely nothing about them. I have to say that all the meditating and visualizations in the world won't pay the bills or put food on the table. You have to do something too – hear the Call to action. When my clients do hear the Call, I challenge them by asking, 'And how are you going to sabotage yourself?' Their old ways of thinking or behaving have been so comfortable, it is easy to be drawn back. They are not even aware that is what they are doing – not coming into reality.

Visible Woman Exercise

- How do you sabotage yourself?

- Take your time responding as it may not be as clear as you think.

- When you have this awareness, simply allow it to sink in. This is what gets in your way of taking action.

Something else that gets in the way of us taking action is when you get bogged down with the clutter – not just in your mind but in your home. So have a spring clean whatever time of the year it is. You can get help from a professional or friends. Do it drawer by drawer, room by room, whatever works for you but do it. This will clear up space in the house and also inside of you.

Visible Woman Exercise

- Looking at your clutter, what is it that stops you from clearing some of it out?

- When you decide to have a clear out, what is it you want to keep?

- What is it you want to discard?

- Think about your reason for both.

Perhaps we hold onto things from the past for a reason. In my introduction, I said that most of us got our sense of identity or a feeling of respect through our role or job title. When this role is taken away, you can be left with a sense of emptiness. This can make you feel invisible and unimportant. This happened to me when I resigned from my position as a director of a training organisation. I felt cast adrift from my colleagues, my roles, my various titles. Not a good place to be. It is useful to remember this when people in our lives lose their job or partner, retire or get ill. We usually don't allow ourselves to acknowledge our feelings of loss, nor do we always realise how much they effect others.

We're all too busy – sometimes we don't even know what or why we're doing what we're doing. It means that we are often too tired to enjoy our family and friends. Remember you looked at the first exercise on how you spend your week in Chapter 1. Were you surprised at where your time went? Well I know some who realise that they simply go round in circles keeping busy. You must know those (if not yourself) who, when there's a great opportunity, somehow can't take it up because there are habits or routines they just always have to do.

Visible Woman Exercise

- What story are you telling yourself about how busy you are?
- Are you just going round in circles?
- (At the very least this exercise may raise a wry smile at what you are doing.)
- How could you 'reclaim' some time for good and pleasurable things?

Sometimes we are so busy trying to be someone else that we forget to ask ourselves, 'what is wrong with simply being me?' We are trying to be the perfect all round woman or reaching for others' standards without appreciating ourselves for what and how we are. Do you actually know anyone who is this goddess you are aspiring to? No, neither do I in real life but let's do this next exercise.

Visible Woman Exercise

- If you don't want to be you, who do you want to be?
- What can you incorporate of that person in your life?
- You may discount you already have the qualities you want to bring into your life and just don't know it yet.

Distractions

Often we use addictions for distraction from our issues whether it's through boredom, fear, worry or feelings of vulnerability. We numb ourselves as we live in a vulnerable world. But your chosen behaviour only works for a little while whether it is eating, drinking, drugs, gambling or sex. That's why you keep on doing it as it triggers the release of feel-good chemicals like serotonin and dopamine. It stops you from being inspired and taking action, and that's why you usually sit on the sidelines. I feel it would be important right now to do the next exercise, before we move on.

Visible Woman Exercise

- If you take the Call (action), what is the worst possible outcome that could happen?

- What is the best possible outcome?

- If you ignore it (stay on the sidelines), what is the worst possible outcome?

- What is the best possible outcome?

You know yourself best so play to your strengths and not your weaknesses. You've less to prove now. You may still want to achieve a lot but you've already done plenty within the confines of your life. The pressure is off. Listen to your life experience, your wisdom and then work out what the Call is. Remember whatever it is can be taken in small steps or a jump.

Stop taking yourself and life so seriously. It causes unnecessary stress and worry. The ability to laugh at life allows us to relate in a more balanced way. After all, what is wrong with being you? When you are overwhelmed, you may need to be on the sidelines and just be for a time. And sometimes you may need a helping hand to take that Call to action. There are those you can turn to for that help.

CHAPTER 5

WRONG NUMBER?
Make the right connection and come home to yourself

✳

*"Thirty-five is when you finally get your head together
and your body starts falling apart"*

CARYN LESCHEN

When you became aware of your Call, did you think you had a wrong number? Those times when we didn't hear what was being said, or the person who answered was not who we expected. The connection was not right or we were not ready for it. We couldn't hear it because we were not living the life we want to live. Or when life was just too overwhelming, out of control and we couldn't cope anymore. Did you connect with 'Is this you?' at the beginning of the book?

No wonder we don't always make the right connection and come home to ourselves. From both my work and home life, I sometimes cannot believe what people have had to overcome in their lives. To keep going is an extraordinary feat in itself and demonstrates human resilience. It is an act of courage to confront our fear of living, taking one day at a time and carrying on anyway. Few of us truly acknowledge and appreciate ourselves for facing our fears. As I've mentioned, I have apprehension about speaking in public and yet my work entails this. So I am acknowledging my courage and I know it is the right connection to myself.

Visible Woman Exercise

- List all the acts of courage you've made by feeling the fear and doing it anyway.

- Allow them into your heart and let them rest there.

- It is always good to remember how brave we are just \ to live life.

I've made many wrong calls and connections. Some have caused distress for me and others. Other times, I can look back and laugh, shake my head, shrug my shoulders and say, 'What was I thinking?'

Visible Woman Exercise

- What wrong numbers have you made in your life?

- What was the effect of these?

- What were the right connections you made?

- How did these affect your life?

As a psychologist, I've been amazed at how many people give up on their dreams. Those dreams you have been afraid of giving freedom to. Remember good things are possible when you do reconnect with them. You can come home to yourself and know that you are more than ordinary, you are extraordinary when you risk doing the things you want to do. You took your courage in both hands and leapt into the unknown by reading this book. You knew you would have to face yourself. You were guided by your Wise Woman or intuition.

I've listened to my intuition a lot in my life. I know there is a part of me much wiser than me. This is my Wise Woman. At times, I've leapt into the unknown and, yes, I've had to contend with other's disapproval sometimes too. However, remember you have the power to decide what's important to you – it's your call. If you believe in yourself then others will too.

Visible Woman Exercise

● Take your time to reflect on who believes in you?

● How does that feel when you let it in?

● Savour the connection with yourself.

Here is Carole's story on how she made the right connection and came home to herself:

Carole's story

'The day that changed the course of my life is etched forever in my mind. I woke on a bright sunny morning knowing that my life was going to be different. The quiet voice inside had a reassuring tone to it and now I had to take action. I knew that the decision I had made was one that I was entirely happy with, albeit fraught with problems.

I had decided that I no longer wanted to be married to my husband. Not that he had done anything wrong; I just knew that a married life with him was not for me.

'I cast my mind back four years, and remembered how I pleaded with my father not to walk me down the aisle; I knew then that it was a big mistake. "You've made your bed and now you have to lie in it," he said. He had always been one for sayings. My parents had both recently remarried and neither of them wanted responsibility for me or my sister. I chose an early marriage to escape and, aged 15, my sister chose to get pregnant. In line with her plan she was thrown out and went to live with her 17 year-old boyfriend. Happily they have now been married for nearly 30 years!

'My thoughts were interrupted by the sound of my three

young children coming into the bedroom. As I looked at them I wondered if I would change my mind. I didn't. The thought of bringing them up by myself was thrilling, this was the happiest I had been for years.

'Naturally, the whole family was disgusted with me. My husband was devastated and threatened all sorts of things. The separation was difficult but I made sure that he had his fair share and arranged a rented house for him to move into. We sold our house and with a tiny amount of money I settled into a new life with my children.

'The next few years were tough but I was free. I chose not to live on maintenance or be a "benefits" mum and started a very small business from home.

'By the end of the fifth year of trading my tenacity and steadfast approach to personal, family and business life was recognised and I became a winner in the national Business Woman of the Year awards.

'After a couple of false starts in new relationships and seeing the hurt in my children I knew I couldn't put them through that again. So, for their sake I put my search for "the ideal man" on hold until my youngest left home. Three months before she was due to go on her gap year and when I was least expecting it, I met a man.

'I'm not really a romantic but when our eyes met something happened. It was at a social event in Church with a friend and he asked if he and his friends could share our table! I can tell you that within seconds of us meeting we had each run through our own "qualifying" checklists and he ticked all the boxes! We married 12 months later and have been married for 10 years now.'

Many of us, unlike Carole, don't make the right connection and come home to ourselves. Why? Usually it's because we are not accepting of ourselves. We've become invisible to ourselves and are not acknowledging the wisdom of ageing. Somewhere we know, but have done so much that we have forgotten that connection.

Erik Erikson, a leader in the field of human social development, maintained that there are particular 'tasks' each of us must tackle at each life stage in order to make the right connection with ourselves. He said that we have to learn not to identify any longer with an ego that has usefully propelled us as young adults into the world of cut and thrust. The world that tells us we're invincible. At mid-life, he maintained, we reach the 'adulthood' phase when we need to assimilate life's experiences and come to accept ourselves.

This is really important to making yourself visible. It's the time we realise the fact that we are not invincible – we will die. All the running around can be a way to avoid the reality that we are slowly moving towards death. One of the ways we do this is to behave as teenagers for as long as we can. It's time to grow up and be the adult we are. You may know some who are still living out their life as teenagers (could even be one yourself!) in their thoughts and actions.

We have to let go of some of our youthful dreams and motivations, in order to grow up. This is in order to re-look and re-assess them for the next stage of our life. Our driving ego-led impulses must be reined in so that we can find ways to achieve a more self-contained, accepting state.

Visible Woman Exercise

- What dreams and motivations do you need to re-assess?
- Are there any you want to bring into reality?
- How will they manifest differently?
- Allow yourself time to be with those possibilities.

Jung saw mid-life as something akin to a second adolescence:

'It is a sort of second puberty, not infrequently accompanied by tempests of passion, the dangerous age'. But Jung also believed that the greatest potential for growth is in the second half of life. He recognised, like Erikson, that to carry on with the same goals we had when we were younger can make us feel rejected; failures; burnt-out. So you need to find a way to stop looking backwards. It's time to look to who and what you can become.

Another way of looking at our lives, is to see if the building of our value system is meeting our needs. American psychologist, Abraham Maslow, built his theory of the hierarchy of needs around the idea that each of us is driven to fulfil whatever the most pressing needs are at different stages in our development.

As you grow into adulthood, you strive to attain love and an identity that allows you a comfortable place in society. You concern yourself with building self-esteem through things such as career and status. When these needs have been met and you can accept who you are, you become more comfortable in your own skin. Maslow called this 'self-actualisation' which is achieving a sense of completeness. This is making the right connection and allowing yourself to be the person you are comfortable with. The one you can look in the mirror and say, 'I really do like you.'

When you allow yourself to be you, you are taking your power. Let me make it clear that taking your power is not about having power over others. It's about setting boundaries and acting on behalf of your own needs in a way that doesn't cause harm to others. In order to take power, you have to be clear about what you feel and think of the people and situations that affect your life. You need to take time to clarify your thoughts and feelings.

The Visible Woman

- When have you felt most at home or comfortable within yourself and who you are?

- What qualities or feelings were you able to express at those times?

- Allow yourself to fully enjoy those experiences.

The occasions when you have felt most comfortable within yourself could be when you have stood your ground without feeling 'bad'. Or when it was right for you to shrug your shoulders and walk away; when it genuinely was of no consequence to you, one way or another. Or those times when you felt at peace with yourself and the world.

Sometimes you can have a broad vision of how life *could* be and of the immense potential of human existence. It is the gap between how it could be and the reality of how it is that causes us pain and leads up to disconnection from ourselves.

What we normally strive to do in life is to develop our ego strength, build our personality and function well, even successfully, in the world. At some stage, the meaning this gives you can start to disappear. You desperately try to recapture this by working more intensely, change jobs, houses, relationships, use substances or holidays to find out what's missing. Underlying this need could be a sense of boredom or aridity and meaninglessness. You are running away from an existential crisis. This can be both a painful time in our lives and yet it also offers the chance to step into new shoes that don't quite fit us yet but will come to.

Most of us aspire to realise our potential and, at the same time, need to deal with patterns of behaviour that prevent this from happening. A crisis can occur when we've had a deep transpersonal or spiritual experience. We see the potential of how the world can be and then return to our daily life and have to deal with the consequences of what we see. We can find it very painful and intolerable. We can get so angry with the world and find living in it unbearable. Our challenge is to be simultaneously rooted and open to the spiritual aspect of life. Some of us may need to take time out from life for a while, and others may be able to cultivate both the horizontal (every day) and vertical (spiritual) aspects of growth.

The dilemmas through life's course; when we are young, when we are successful adults, during mid-life, and as we become old, are often characterised literally or metaphorically by questions about meaning. What's the point of life? What am I here for? I've got everything I need and still it is not enough. The striving for success no longer satisfies an inner deeper need. A colleague and I ran courses called 'I'm successful – so what?' The course dealt with these questions of meaning and was pretty challenging for some of the participants.

Let's hear from a woman who was questioning life and whether what she was doing was enough:

Lynne's story

'About six years ago I wanted to make changes in my life, particularly to lose weight, but something more was nagging away at me. I listened and had to acknowledge that I was bored – I was not being stretched enough and needed more in my life. I became a Virtual Assistant and loved doing that – lots of fun. Unfortunately though there was a family crisis which made me look again at my life. This time I realised that I wanted to do more for others.

'I decided to raise £50,000 in a year for young people who have cancer so that all the best facilities were in place to make their journey easier than it is. After a big learning curve, I got the hang of fundraising and actually raised £54,000. I love all the new skills I have learned – from trekking in the Himalayas, learning to ride a bike, speaking in public, organising events and making my own website.

'My life is very different now and that doesn't mean better, just different. I love it and I love helping others. I think I was meant to do this. Taking time and trusting my intuition or my inner wisdom, my life is full and fulfilling.

'There's a wonderful saying which goes something like, "It's

an issue of age over matter – if you don't mind, it doesn't matter'.

'The young people I meet with cancer have taught me not to worry about next week, or next year, to enjoy today, right now. It's all any of us have after all – right now.
We submitted our application to be a Scottish charity and my goal is to raise £1million in the next two years. And you know what? I will do it.'

What a woman! Here is extraordinariness being enacted in the ordinariness of life. There's nothing better than being in the presence of someone with a cheerful heart, like Lynne. You can't help feeling graced by their positive energy. It's easy to have a long face – there's plenty to be upset about in life if we choose to dwell in that place. Why not instead look to this kind of person to lift your mood, or better still become more like them even in a small way.

Visible Woman Exercise

- List those you know who lift your spirit.

- What is it about them that brings this about?

- Where is that in you right now?

- You could also ask your friends, 'How do I lift your spirits?'

Extraordinary things begin with ordinary gestures, and your success in life is not about working hard to please others. It comes from you being in a contented emotional state, which then allows you to maximise your effectiveness. For me, this is the feeling when I am aligned with myself. It is not easy and can be short-lived. But I promise you that the times when it is there, life falls into place.

Visible Woman Exercise

- What is the ordinary gesture you are most pleased with in your life?

- What was the effect on others?

- How do you feel when you acknowledge that it didn't take much and yet you were part of a simple gesture?

An example of an ordinary gesture from my own life is that a neighbour of mine holds 'cards and jewellery' parties about three or four times a year. She gets something out of the giving of them, the making of the jewellery and the charities benefit from any profit. And we all enjoy catching up with one another. A win-win situation.

We all have something we want in life. It could be a better job, house, health, happiness, a relationship or peace of mind. The problem is that we can also block ourselves from achieving what we want without even realising that this is what we are doing. Me, for instance, I want to be slimmer and yet I block myself with my love of food!

Visible Woman Exercise

- What is it that you want?

- How do you block yourself from achieving it?

- Or in psychosynthesis we say, 'And how will you sabotage yourself?'

It's better to make friends with your saboteur than pretend it doesn't exist. We all have a part that wants to stop us from fulfilling ourselves. So we might fall and trip, so we won't go to the dance and have fun, we sabotage ourselves unconsciously.

Following with my own example, another of the things I want, is to support you in your quest to improve the quality of your life. I want to encourage you to learn to listen to your inner voice. This can make you calmer in the midst of the chaos of life.

In psychosynthesis, this would be called, coming from the "I", the conscious self which makes decisions and choices. An analogy used is like being the conductor of your own orchestra. You have the baton (your will) and you are in charge of all these parts (subpersonalities) of you. These are the instruments of the orchestra. The conductor (you) can acknowledge the valuable side of any sub-personality, for example, your 'lust' or your 'critic'. It can draw them out or gesture to them to be quiet. It can negotiate how you can retain and use the positive aspect and tone down the abrasive side of any sub-personality. You then play your own music.

Visible Woman Exercise

- When do you feel you are the conductor of your orchestra?

- What are the qualities you were embodying at those times?

- How were you feeling?

- How did the world respond to you?

Your mind and attitude towards life – rather than the acquisition of material possessions – is what is our true source of pleasure. Yes, of course, that lovely meal or those expensive designer shoes will bring a smile to your face. But if you don't get them then you can always cheer yourself up by remembering that enjoyment comes from inside. If you have an approach to life which requires a light touch, the capacity to let go, then your ability to enjoy life is your wealth. I am not saying that money isn't important. Of course it is, especially when you are struggling to pay your bills and keep a roof over your head. I've been there so I know what it's like.

Money is one of the rewards you get for adding value to the lives of others. It is a symbol of your confidence in your service and yourself. When you improve yourself, you are improving the lives of those around us. Your motivation allows you to rekindle your drive and energy for living.

When you think of wealth, it is usual to think of material wealth, freedom from financial worry, or owning a beautiful home.

But this is not an adequate definition of true wealth – it's just one element in a system that makes up a good life. Non-financial assets include your family and friends. Again, wealth is the sense of knowing you are contributing to the world. That your life is worthwhile.

Sometimes we fall short and sometimes we just can't do whatever it is we are striving for. I have found that simply adding 'yet' to the end of 'I haven't done it' takes pressure off me. So see what pressure you can take off yourself today by adding 'Yet'.

Remember you don't have to create a painting, write a book or compose a symphony to make a contribution. Your capacity for spiritual and psychological development is enormous so consider your life to be your creative expression.

Visible Woman Exercise

- What can you do to enhance your understanding of yourself?

- When will you make that time for yourself?

- It is really important for your own well-being that you make this time.

If you're feeling brave enough, you could ask your close friends and/or colleagues for their honest opinion of your strengths and limitations. You can also read self-development and inspirational books, attend courses or write your autobiography so you can see the patterns (good and bad) of your life.

There will be times when we may need to step back in our lives through our own decisions or have one forced upon us. On those occasions, it can be fine that others don't see us, that we are invisible. We can't be acknowledged all the time. When we trust the process and know we are visible to ourselves, life will still give us satisfaction.

One of the ways you may want your call to be a wrong number is when you are under stress. Although some of us thrive on stress and, when it is brief, our motivation can be high and we achieve a sense of achievement. However, when anxiety is prolonged and consistent, good stress turns bad and has seriously damaging effects on health, and behaviour, for example, irritability, sleeping difficulties, panic attacks, tearfulness and depression. As I said earlier, it also exacts a considerable physical toll too. It increases the likelihood of problems ranging from mouth ulcers to heart disease. I know for me that the weight lifts off my shoulders and I feel lighter when I actually tackle what is causing my anxiety and stress. I can breathe deeply again!

Visible Woman Exercise

- What do you need to tackle?

- What support do you need to do it?

- Imagine yourself tackling what's causing you to be stressed. Allow yourself to feel lighter and easier in your body. Then you can use these feelings and bodily reactions to take the steps to tackle the issue.

Remember you are not on your own. You can ask for help. Resilient people are those who are comfortable reaching out and asking for help (and giving it back when it is asked of you) and is one of the healthiest capacities you can develop. There are many resources out there waiting to be connected with which are the right numbers for you

Don't let your passion die – rekindle the flame now. Take that time to reconnect with what it is that makes your heart sing. Your ability to enjoy life is your wealth, however you carry it out. Be more flexible and be open to new ideas. The more you trust yourself – trust the process – the more willing you'll become to invest in life regardless of whether you think it may or may not work out.

CHAPTER 6

RETURNING YOUR CALL
Leave your legacy to the world

'What one can be, one must be'
ABRAHAM MASLOW

It is a truism that we are only here for a short time so we should act and live in a way that reflects positively on our existence. Sounds pretty good to me. And returning our Call is what enables you and me to be part of the bigger picture of helping to make the world the kind of place we want it to be. The Call may be to continue to connect to our spirit as well as doing grounded work in the world. It is about leaving our legacy to the world. But we may not even know if we have actually done anything. Remember one of the ways is by being ourselves and to fulfil our potential.

I recall saying to a colleague, Murray, who showed faith in my recovery by keeping a co-leading team building offer open for me, that I didn't know if I had made a difference in life. He simply responded by reminding me of all the people I'd come in touch with and enabled them to make a difference. Tears flowed freely at this. So let's give you the opportunity to reflect.

Visible Woman Exercise

● What are the ways in which you give back?

● What do you see as your legacy?

● You might be surprised by your answer as it may not be what you expected.

Much of the time society says "One person can't make a difference so why bother?" and, if we listen to that, we will do nothing at all. Having said that, the following poem can offer you a possibility you have not thought about:

> **100 years from now it will not matter**
> **What kind of car I drove**
> **What kind of house I lived in**
> **How much money I had in my bank account**
> **Nor what my clothes looked like**
> **But the world may be a little better**
> **Because I was important in the life of a child.**
> JENNIFER UNLIMITED

So there is also my legacy to my family. You can make a difference through caring for your family, speaking your truth particularly about injustices, volunteering, teaching someone to read, working to the best of your ability, creating or supporting charity organisations, giving without any expectations, and making our environment as good as it can be. These are all part of being human. I see many quietly and even noisily who are making a difference. For me this was through doing charity runs (or walks in my case). Yours can be giving blood, picking up litter in your local streets, becoming a governor at your local school or facing your fear. The last one can make a difference to others as they see you do this, and are inspired by it. You will know what is right for you.

Meaning can be found in very small acts and interactions as well as large ones. I know someone who has chosen to give one of her kidneys to a neighbour without any 'hoo-ha'. Debbie is an exceptional woman who has given a neighbour the gift of life and sees this act as something she chose to do without a fuss. I am proud to know her.

Remember, you can make a difference simply by living your life to the full.

Social scientists say that it only takes 11 per cent of people to transform the world. What about that? Only 11 per cent of us to make a difference. You can take action to remedy wrongs, however small or insignificant, as it contributes to positive change. It lifts you from a sense of hopelessness over children going hungry for example, or global warming, or problems specific to your own community. By changing yourself, you'll feel less powerless and so you can contribute to changing the world.

Here is an example of how one woman's Call enabled her to make a difference to others.

Kristina's story

'I ask myself, can it happen twice in a lifetime? Or is each Call only the preparation for the next one?

'Over 30 years ago, I suddenly had an amazing insight that I'd create a therapy for cancer patients and look at their attitudes towards getting over or accepting it.

'I almost forgot that first Call as my married life was totally on the rocks and I was in so much pain and despair. In my exhaustion, I visited a little 12th century chapel on the River Mosel and asked for help or awareness into what I should do. No answer came but when I was leaving, I saw above the door the words "I have no hands but yours". I suddenly became very sure that the work with cancer patients was meant to be. It was a reminder of my Call. I had my lust for life again.

'When I had accepted the Call, I met the right people, found the right books, came across the right training – even the "right" money to do it all.

'Nowadays, I look back and see what impact and influence my acceptance of the Call had – working with over 2,000 patients with my "Systemic Cancer Care Programme", and training hundreds of good students.

'I am making my knowledge and experience attainable for many through my work. And writing is now on the agenda. I am open for the next Call and next experiences of my life. If it shall be, it will happen.'

Remember most of us have suffered some kind of emotional wound in our life. You are not alone. Who said life would be perfect? You can try to deny your wounds and distance yourself from painful memories or you can get help and heal yourself. When you heal your pain this can turn into your best asset and you can help others. As Oprah Winfrey said, 'Turn your wounds into wisdom'. One definition of wisdom is the thoughtful application of learning.

Visible Woman Exercise

- How have you healed your wound(s)?

- What have you learned from your hard times?

- How has this become an asset that has enabled others?

Sometimes you can just feel like crying, or be so angry at how the world is and how it could be. When those feelings arise, don't hold back or deny them. Allow the sadness, grief, anger or helplessness to be there. They need to be acknowledged before you can move on. Some see this as weakness and say that it should be risen above but I am not of this view. Our vulnerability is also the birthplace of our joy and creativity. Feel what you feel and then decide how to tackle what is bothering you.

The ability to deeply feel enriches our life, making us more compassionate and caring towards others, and this world of ours. It can also be the motivation to bring about change in your and other people's lives.

Visible Woman Exercise

- What could you do with your life that would benefit the generations to come?

- Would you change your day-to-day decisions?

- How can you celebrate this realisation?

Everything makes a difference whether we realise it or not. Kindness also changes us internally too. In his book *Why Kindness is Good for You* David Hamilton explains that,

'Scientific evidence has proven that kindness changes the brain, impacts the heart and immune system, and may even be an antidote to depression. We're actually genetically wired to be kind and that kindness has evolved in us and thus its effects are felt daily throughout the nervous systems. When we're kind, our bodies are healthiest.' What a wonderful incentive!

Visible Woman Exercise

- Make a list of all your kind acts towards yourself this week.

- Make a list of all your kind acts towards others this week.

- Then slowly breathe each one in to replenish you.

It's important to be kind to others, but it's also important to help yourself and relieve any pressure on you by creating a more sane and balanced life. You don't have to do everything people ask of you, that's not kindness, that can wear you down. It's more simple than that: it's when you smile at the shop assistant or ticket collector, when you're kind to your family. This is when you are actually causing changes in your brain chemistry. You are helping to keep yourself healthy!

The American actress, Susan Sarandon said, 'How can you

not participate in the world you live in?' Her challenge to me is to be fully alive, to take part in the life around me, not to keep my passion underground and feel half-alive. Hers is a very good question for us to ponder over, particularly as visible women. Women around the world are becoming financially powerful enough to stand on their own two feet. They can tip the world's power balance, starting with their home life, extending to work and finally affecting society in general. This is not some feminist cry, it's just fact and simple history. We now have the opportunity to influence the workings of the world.

Most of us need to earn a living but the highest motivation for work is to serve others. This can be carried out even when we don't know how we are helping people. It enables you to give the best service you can. Shifting your motivation from money to service makes for a more uplifting, satisfying and rewarding life. Research has shown that it's when you're making a contribution, making a difference for others that you're at your happiest. So generously share your gifts and talents so that we can all benefit.

I was really touched by how American author and poet, Sondra Zeidenstein, shares her legacy in her work:

'I will call my collection: *old woman, new poems.* What else but art can take on this experience of life coming to an ending but lived in the daily? What else can communicate the minute and extreme changes that mark the drama of old age, this strange intensity of absence foreshadowed in presence?

These things matter: to keep going, to keep writing, making our art, or whatever brings us all the way out into the world, our print on the consciousness of the earth, of each other. I want to be known for who I am as an old woman artist. I want to be in the conversation. It's as simple as that.'

What an honest woman whose work will touch generations to come. Her words will resonate with others and therefore make her visible.

Another woman who has made herself visible in the world is Esther Rantzen. She identifies two proverbs as her inspiration to take action for the causes and people she cares about:

> **'If I am not for me, who will be? If I am only for me, what am I? If not now, when?'**
> RABBI HILLEL

> **'For the triumph of evil it is only necessary that good men do nothing'**
> EDMUND BURKE

Maybe we can't all have the drive, enthusiasm and passion of Esther but we can still offer our version. Again, you don't have to create a painting, write a book or compose a symphony to be creative. Your capacity for spiritual and psychological development is enormous so consider your life to be your creative expression. If you have skills and knowledge consider sharing them as a teacher. The world needs good teachers who are mature and who have life experience as well as knowledge.

Perhaps reading this book is one of the ways you are enhancing your understanding of yourself, your psychology and spirituality.

Your unique contribution can be known by turning inward and listening to your inner voice, that Call, and asking:

Visible Woman Exercise

- Why am I here?

- What is mine to do in this world?

- You may be surprised at what arises when you are open to the answer. And it may be, Simply Be Yourself and do what you can.

Although it was a tremendous generous act of giving (some may say foolhardy), you don't need to be like Kevin Salwen and his family who sold their luxurious American family home, donated half of the proceeds to charity and used the other half to buy a more modest replacement home. The aim of this family was not actually to get people to sell their houses but to encourage people to step off the treadmill of accumulation, to define themselves by what they give as well as by what they possess. The family certainly left their legacy. Their book, *The Power of Half*, chronicles the project.

We need to leave a legacy for others to draw upon. It is important that you draw on your inner resources of wisdom and compassion (the feminine principle in psychosynthesis is right brain thinking) as these are the key forces at play in the healing of our world.

Here is someone who, after searching for an answer to 'There must be more to life than this. What is it?' is leaving her legacy to the world.

Janet's story

The beginning of a "wake-up" call to life was when I'd had a spiritual experience after my mother died suddenly and unexpectedly while I was home from university. This difficult experience had a great gift of love within it which has resounded down the years.

'After my third son died just before he was born, I began searching for an answer to "There must be more to life than this. What is it?" All sorts of subtle changes and opportunities came my way after I asked this question.

'My working life was dedicated to teaching science in state

secondary schools. Later I began helping at a cancer support group whilst training as a Healer. Working with people dealing with cancer changed me and impacted out into the world.

'One example was when I refused to teach in a new purpose built science laboratory for six months because it was not safe. This was supported and eventually ended in positive results for the school. Another was a tough situation that we, as a family, endured for some 20 years which cost us dearly financially, mentally and spiritually. And although, even now life is not easy, the inner mantra "I can and will do this" kicks in and helps.

'I now work as a counsellor part-time with an agency that specialises in working with children, families and parents. And the rest of my time is taken up working with an International Creative Meditation Group. And gradually a strength and resourcefulness has come from my knowing there is more to life than my everyday experiences.

'I also revel in knowing that you only have to know six other people to be in contact with – directly or indirectly – all the other people in the planet – a lovely, lovely fact! This connection can help to change the world.'

Janet has connected with herself, faced her fears and allowed her happiness out. Another point of interest is Maeve Haran's *Daily Mail* article responding to a survey on 'What makes you really happy'. It showed that what really gave her pleasure in life were the small things – good bread, warm towels, laughing babies, fresh coffee and old friends.

At the top of the survey, guess what? A good night's sleep! I can just hear my son and daughter-in-law, parents of young children, saying 'Yes' to that and many others too with young children. Maeve Haran was stunned at how many of the things that make us all happy don't cost a thing. More valuable than wealth and far more useful than designer handbags are the people who bring the laugher, support and dedication to your life.

Visible Woman Exercise

- What are your simple free pleasures?

- What makes you really happy? Make a list

- Take time to allow these in and really appreciate them.

- Any surprises?

If you can pay your bills and keep the wolf from the door, you may be surprised at how little you need to be happy. Others have also said freshly baked bread, clean bed-sheets, holding grandchildren, making snowmen, letting other drivers into traffic, de-cluttering. Your discovery may be that your simple pleasures don't cost you anything either. Whenever you need to, remember Maeve Haran's list, and the one you did for yourself. Nothing boosts your confidence more than being happy.

Consider too, happiness robbery. When you live in fear of something, small or large, known or unknown, or tolerate something in your life you don't want, this can create the most anxiety. This is the low-level type of anxiety that causes you to numb yourself with too much wine or rubbish TV night after night. You're anaesthetising yourself with food, alcohol, cigarettes or TV. It takes great courage to take the steps to deal with that anxiety because it is painful as well as scary. When you are scared to make a change, know you're scared but do it anyway: this is what is known as 'feel the fear and do it anyway'. I have mentioned this earlier in the book and it is important to re-visit it.

Visible Woman Exercise

- Make a list of all the things you would do if you felt the fear and did it anyway.

- Choose one.

- When will you take the first step towards it?

- What support might you need?

- Remember there are professionals who can help as well as your circle of friends and family.

Why feel the fear? Why not avoid it? Because it's no good trying to get rid of fear. It's a natural survival response which is part of our make-up. We're biologically programmed for it. It triggers a flight or fight response from the ancient reptilian part of our brain which floods our body with stress hormones: cortisone and adrenaline. These would be useful if you had to fight or run away from a predator. They aren't much help when you're tossing and turning in bed worrying about something that you've probably blown out of proportion. As our fear increases, our ability to think rationally decreases.

The bad news is that there doesn't seem to be any way to stop this part of the brain from broadcasting fear impulses. The good news is that you can light up other parts of your brain instead – such as the left pre-frontal love cortex, a region associated with contentment. But it does take a bit of brain training and commitment to using tools that can quickly switch our brain from fear to calm.

According to medical psychologists, it is neurologically impossible for your brain to create emotions such as gratitude and appreciation while simultaneously feeling afraid. Courage is a massively underrated virtue. Remember you have courage muscles behind your fear so try them out.

Someone who pushed at the boundaries of courage and fear is Anne. Here's what she writes:

Anne's story

'I feel inspired by James Hillman's quote, "We blame our parents for our wounds; Our wounds therefore parent us; Hence our wounds are the parents of our destinies." I hold this difficult concept in the context of my personal and universal suffering.

'I was born to parents who were themselves in a deep crisis of meaning, one suffering from depression and the other deep shame. My father committed suicide when I was three months old and my mother was hospitalised in a psychiatric hospital until I was two years old. I was abandoned but was rescued by generous, spirited, Scottish Highland people who sowed the seeds of love and service in me.

'I was very identified with being a survivor as I found out during my later therapy. I had to take on too much responsibility at a very young age. My mother descended into another deep depression and at 14 years old, formal education wasn't a possibility any more. I became a hairdresser and wanted to travel. I married at 19 and moved to England where the striving in me brought many riches. I had made it. I had everything I could want including a family but I became depressed. This evoked all the old shame of visiting my mother in mental institutions.

'This time also evoked anger and I knew I had no choice but to agree to see an art therapist at a local mental hospital. He told me, "You don't belong here in this environment." It took courage to be open to this. He introduced me to a model of psychospiritual psychotherapy called psychosynthesis.

'Many years of rich learning have passed. I now pass on my strong will to be of service, as was modelled by the kindly neighbours who cared for me. I have been enabled to give something back. I continue to teach and supervise others and have also founded my own centre. This centre, in the heart of the City of London, has the quality of a sanctuary for people to rest awhile.

'I am at a new stage in my life which I have experienced

with wonder and gratitude. My children are grown and we've been blessed with two grandchildren. I also have much love, support and gratitude to the man I have been with for 46 years.

'I am so pleased that I returned my "Calls" and am leaving my legacy to the world.'

Anne, was the woman who found me standing on the corner doing market research. Her legacy has definitely spread far and wide through me, and others she came in contact with.

Our society doesn't seem to acknowledge that it takes courage to look at ourselves and our life. Especially when you realise you're becoming invisible and your wounds may be too painful to acknowledge. When you do stop though, wake up and give yourself the time you so deserve, so that you can start becoming more visible again to the most important person - yourself.

You also begin to see why the term middle-age has become meaningless. You no longer conform to rules that once accorded to your chronological age. You push at the boundaries of what was once called middle-age.

Being in the second half of life, you can be young enough to get more out of it, old enough to have experience and mature enough to laugh at it and yourself. You might find you've achieved that magical life-stage where giving gives you as much happiness as taking.

Visible Woman Exercise

- When, and with whom, do you get enjoyment out of giving?

- What do you feel inside?

- Allow yourself to be with those feelings. Remember you can always reconnect with them whenever you want.

Here is some advice from an American Psychologist, Richard

Carlson, on how to live life. He begins with the very important message of, 'treasure yourself, you're precious.' He goes on to say that living in the present allows you to be wholly with people, or what you're doing, so that you can make most of it.

But this can be a long journey, and as we're only human there's nothing wrong with having self-doubt. Whatever your self-doubt is, it really can hold you back in life and stop you from realising your potential. Mine is not feeling good enough but it still does not have the power to stop me. Nowadays, I can say that I am enough. I no longer need to strive for perfection. I am a good enough person as I am.

The most powerful thing is to *stop* when you feel over-crowded or over-whelmed and give yourself space. One of the ways to do this is by meditating, which I mentioned earlier in the book. Meditation as used in psychosynthesis, can be defined as a form of inner action. Far from being an escape from life or to stop the mind, the point of meditation is to be present, to cultivate awareness. Put another way, it could simply be seen as stopping, taking a deep breath and just being.

These moments of stillness give us the opportunity to listen to our inner wisdom. The stress of modern life gives us little time to regenerate. We seldom create moments of quiet reflection, of just being. I am guilty of forgetting to do this at times. And remember that absorbing activities can act as a meditation for you.

Another way for you to connect with that inner quiet is to allow yourself to have a symbol of something to remind you of, for example, how much you are loved, supported, appreciated and even applauded for being you. This can be a piece of jewellery, a photo, a quote or something that is meaningful to you. Whether you reconnect to your choice externally in the future, you will have already unconsciously connected internally.

Visible Woman Exercise

- What would you choose as a symbolic reminder of simply being you?

- How can you bring this into your life?

- This will also reflect your visibility to yourself.

Remember that you matter, being yourself matters, your participation in the world matters. You are so important. Therefore return your Call and be visible in the world. This is your legacy to us all.

What one can be one must be, sums up this chapter. This is your time – take it and others will benefit from your legacy. Allow the world to see that your being or doing is your choice now. Your family and friends will tell you when you are taking yourself too seriously. When you believe You are enough then you will listen to your Wise Woman.

CHAPTER 7

THE CALL OF YOUR WISE WOMAN

Celebrate, have fun and be visible

*'The more you praise and celebrate your life,
the more there is in life to celebrate'*

OPRAH WINFREY

This is the Call of your Wise Woman to listen to yourself and others, to express and be visible in the world, to make a difference in others' lives, to play and have fun. To sum it up, celebrate being alive. Aren't we so lucky to still be here and have all these possibilities ahead of us?

Celebration for me is quite simply that I am alive and living life. As I was recovering from surgery, the realisation that I wanted the freedom of getting out and about again in my car was when I knew my energy had come back. I was still part of life by going out to play, having fun, and laughing at life from the belly. I could begin to focus on the wider world again – not just me. Life was so much sweeter and beautiful.

Visible Woman Exercise

- What are the many ways in which you celebrate life?

- What are you doing today to celebrate?

- Remember to do it with passion.

Life can throw so much at us. There's no way all will be serene and peaceful forever more – even if we wish it could be. Your feelings are part of your reality – no more denial. Listening to them, acknowledging them and choosing whether you express them or not is a whole different ball game than pushing them away. The ups and downs of life (painful and joyful) are part of our life's journey. The more you pretend otherwise, the more crazy you can become.

Recall all that you have in your 'bank' to draw upon to cope with life. Remembering my friend's knock on the door many years ago and say. 'Can you come out to play?' still makes me smile outside and inside, and I feel good. Also the daft things I've done, and my family, grandchildren and friends. These are what I have in my bank to draw upon.

I have so much to be grateful for – my openness, the people I know and have known, and people I have yet to meet. This is the time of the Visible Woman, and including my wisdom and life experience.

Visible Woman Exercise

- Take time to imagine you're holding a gratitude party simply for being alive.

- Who would you invite?

- How would you decorate your house/venue for this celebration?

- What would you wear to it?

- What are the things you are grateful for?

- Take time to breathe all of this gratitude in.

Oh, how most of us take ourselves too seriously. We all do it! We can drown in shame if we make a mistake or cling to an inflated or rigid view of ourselves. Life is much easier if you can step back once in a while and laugh at yourself. Go for a walk, take time out, and have a good laugh at your own expense. You'll gain a much better perspective on life.

Don't beat yourself up with what you read here and haven't done. My words are here to inspire you – nothing more, or else you'll feel oppressed. Make a note of suggestions and ideas you want to try and let the others go. You can then try to integrate the ideas that appeal most into your life in your own way. If things don't work out, don't take them too seriously or lose heart. Try something else that's worthy of your lust for life.

Remember to look for your lust in unlikely places – no matter how impractical, insignificant or even grand it seems. Then begin to honour your passion and bring it to the centre of your life.

Visible Woman Exercise

- What really excites you or fires you up?

- Where is it now, that passion?

- Really feel it in your body and then make a commitment to allow it in each day.

Once you allow your passion in again, you'll find you will take risks. You'll have courage to follow your heart's desire – the call of the Wise Woman. It's not about playing it safe as this can lead to boredom and depression. Remember I said previously that when we are not stretched enough or challenged to move out of our comfort zone, we can become depressed. Who chooses that? We have choices in whether we climb mountains, take time out, go sailing, write a book, make a documentary, learn to dance, go on retreats, visit other countries, enjoy our families or simply be still.

When you succeed you can inspire others. Even when it doesn't quite work out as planned, you've still challenged yourself and will grow from what you've learned. When you change your life so that it's more in line with what inspires you, you can share what you learn with others. Trust your inner wisdom, your voice, your visibility that it is valuable to the world.

Here is the story of a woman who discovered she could inspire others:

Sharon's story

'I became a single parent by the time I was 20 years old. Life was tough and there were times I went without food in order for us both to survive. But my determination helped me to learn shorthand and typing in three months and, over time I built my career to management level.

'I married but it turned out to be an unhappy marriage. Although separated, I decided to stay in the marriage as I now had a second child. This was to help the family get through a financial crisis. I divorced in my late 40's and was once again a single parent.

'Having trained as a psychotherapist, and later as a coach and trainer, I even went on to triumphantly gain a Master's degree in Psychotherapy at 53 years old.

'Throughout all my problems and challenges, I have been passionate about developing myself to be the most I can be and to pass my learning onto others. Now at 62 years old, I have fulfilled another lifetime's dream by becoming an author. I am so content with my loving family, grandchildren and friends and see life as an adventure full of possibilities.'

Your contentment is your real wealth and, just like Sharon, it's about expressing gratitude for the life you have. It is a state of mind and doesn't depend on anything external. You enjoy owning material possessions but you don't let them own you. This inner peace can also evoke a lovely feeling of excitement. It's your Call that leads you to do things that will make you content.

Regardless of what life presents – good or bad – the way

you respond makes all the difference. Life is never fair. People face disability, loss, abandonment, redundancy or you may have a collection of ordinary problems that simply make life difficult. This is when we can draw on our inner peace and regard life's difficulties as a challenge, and even an opportunity once we've begun to recover from the initial crisis. But sometimes this can take some time.

Therefore, bring all your intelligence, passion and abilities to bear in creating the best life you can. When you're ready to, take inspiration from those who have overcome adversity, in whatever form, and triumphed. Look at Oprah Winfrey's story to see what she has triumphed over. Her early life wasn't easy, but she has kept her sense of humour; as she says, 'I still have my feet on the ground, I just wear better shoes.'

What would it be like to be satisfied with what you have in this moment? You probably haven't even thought about that! Your ego makes you feel you're centre of your universe. But that continual self-absorption can get you into trouble by creating negative emotions. Try to lessen your focus on yourself and move your focus towards appreciating life.

The author, Dominique Browning, wrote that in the aftermath of an out-of-work crisis, she reconnected with 'the desire to nourish my soul.' She began to appreciate what she describes as the 'small beauty in every single day'. We should also seek this appreciation in how we play. As someone said, 'You don't stop playing because you grow old, you grow old because you stop playing.'

Visible Woman Exercise

- What are the many ways you bring play into your life?

- If you've forgotten, how are you going to remember?

- What will you do today?

Adults need to play, to have fun, be creative, experience joy and continue to learn. Yet it can be easy to forget how to. You can begin to play more with your own or others' children, your pets, your partner. It's great to have your grandchildren to play with. Or simply laugh at life. Look at my 101+ things I've learned at the back of the book for inspiration.

Laughter is medicine for the soul. William James said, "We don't laugh because we're happy, we're happy because we laugh." Laugh at yourself and life as you get older. Greet it with fun and reflection in between moaning and groaning about ageing. And, most importantly, celebrate your life. By celebrating you'll find the energy to deal with what is not working. Also you can give back into life what life has given and supported you in accomplishing.

We don't have to be the Polyanna's in life though. Here, I am saying don't try and be positive all the time because it'll exhaust you. And it will certainly annoy others. Listen to yourself and allow or acknowledge what you're feeling, for example, if sad then be sad. All our feelings are part of our celebration of life. The joy of being alive more than the fear of death is what enables us to change.

For Roberto Assagioli, amongst others in the human potential movement, there was an innate developmental tendency within each of us to actualise our potential, to become what we are capable of becoming. Therefore, play to your strengths or another way is to honour what you have rather than what you don't have. When you have pulled all this together, ask yourself the deeper question of, 'Now how can I use what I have discovered in my life?' Simply wait and see over the next days or weeks whether an answer comes in.

There's a Hindu saying that says, 'Any worthwhile activity, however ordinary – but done in the right spirit – takes us one step closer to happiness.' So how about taking everyday moments and making them pleasurable. If there is only you for lunch, then set the tray or table as if you were expecting a special friend. And if you're not pouring yourself some wine, then at least put your soft drink into a lovely glass and enjoy. That'll bring a smile to your face. Go back to your 'what makes you really happy' list you made earlier in the book, and see what you've written. Some get pleasure from stepping into a warm bath with lovely warm towels to come out to. Something I love is battling against the wind on the seafront (wearing the right clothes of course, I'm not such a masochist). It is so invigorating and makes you feel alive. Also others out doing the same thing (usually with their dogs) always smile and acknowledge you. We're simply people enjoying life.

Visible Woman Exercise

- What everyday activity can you allow yourself to get pleasure from?

- When will you do it?

One thing I have learned was is to be happy you have to be willing to give up all hopes for a better past. Only then can you truly get on with your life.

I remember being told, 'You should never regret your past. All that matters is where you are now and where you are going. The past, with all its ups and downs, is what made you.' So self-acceptance of how you've turned out because of, or in spite of, what you have had to learn from your past is so important.

When I began my therapy training and was asked what was the basis of my work, I answered that it was about helping clients to accept themselves as they are, with all the parts of them. My therapist enabled me to see that I could accept myself with both the good parts and the parts I didn't want to acknowledge. This enabled me to feel lighter and freer to develop and move forwards on my journey.

You'll have heard people (if not yourself) ask any number of versions of, 'Don't I have the right to be happy?' And the combined wisdom of the ages might respond, 'No, you have to earn it, work towards it, be deserving of it, come across it on the course of your search for meaning.'

Happiness is you – your original nature. It is how you feel when you accept and are true to yourself. Good things are possible; so take the time now and listen to your Inner Voice or Call. I encourage you to be brave, take your courage in both hands and risk doing the things you want to do. If you say *Yes* first, you can always say *No* later, but if you say *No* to begin with, you'll never know what you missed, will you?

Professor Martin Seligman founded the Positive Psychology movement after a life working on disabling conditions such as depression, suicide and schizophrenia. He says that wanting to be happy is different from *not* wanting to be depressed. It's not about going around with a big smile on your face. Professor Seligman goes on to say that 'Happiness equals positive emotion (pleasant life), positive character (engaged life) and positive institutions (meaningful life). We're hive creatures and we feel the *need to belong and serve something bigger*. We need to use our higher strengths and talents to meet the challenges that confront us.' I think he and I are on the same track with our views on life.

When your passion and enthusiasm drives you into action, your goal(s) can need the co-operation of others. It will make your life much easier if you get them onboard. If this doesn't happen, then still go for it and motivate yourself. Remember you're taking the steps to move dreams out of your head and into reality. You will be using your talents and expressing your passion to make a difference in today's world, which is so badly needed. Others will enjoy them too.

Amarita is a model example of using passion and enthusiasm. Here is her story:

Amarita's story

'*My story starts about 15 years ago with a leap of faith, an inner impulse, which caused me to buy a one way ticket to Seville. I was searching for something without really knowing what it was that I was there to find. As I peeked inside a small doorway in the old quarter of Santa Cruz, I fell instantly and completely in love with the music, dance and song; the commotion of tables knocked over and glasses smashed to the floor. I had a "eureka" moment. This was a turning point. Somehow I must have known that it was waiting. My journey into Flamenco challenged, and still challenges, all of my resistance, fears and insecurities. It is a furnace in which the self is refined and purified – but not before going through a huge amount of physical, mental and emotional struggle.*

'*As a child, I was always tall for my age which grew into teenage awkwardness. I had no pride in my femininity and wore baggy, formless clothes. I developed a stooped posture. I channelled my energy into academic excellence – eventually going to Oxford to start a PhD. My first big shift was to drop my PhD to focus on my creative life which caused consternation to friends and family. I knew it was the right thing to do although on the outside it looked as if I was giving up the opportunity to have a brilliant, prestigious career.*

'*I started a long, long road of what many call discipline but which in fact has more to do with devotion. The internal impulse was strong and carried me over ten years of faithfully travelling to my classes.*

'*Over time I grew more self-aware and stronger. I noticed changes in my posture – far more upright, confident and assertive - and I found a naturalness in expressing myself through the physicality of the body. I found a vehicle for channelling my spirit and expressing emotion in the intensity of the moment. I became more dynamic, radiant and expressive.*

'I am often amazed when I stand in front of a class as a role model and remember how I felt at the beginning of my process with Flamenco. I see my former self in the faces of my students. Flamenco still carries me onward to new lands and experiences. The journey is never completed. I dance on knowing that it will be with me forever.

'I am so, so pleased I listened to that inner impulse. This is my celebration of being visible in the world.'

What a wonderful, inspiring story for each of us. Many years of hard work and yet Amarita's inner call supported her.

Each of us in our own way needs to celebrate or acknowledge every day, or even just once a week, what we have done towards our vehicle of expression in the world. You might get a big surprise. Also remember to celebrate others so there is an abundance going around.

Visible Woman Exercise

- What opportunities/resources do I have that I haven't even noticed before?

- Who do I already know that could help me?

- What do I know but have never thought could help?

- What does the voice of my wise woman tell me?

Know you *can* do it. If not you, then who? Don't undermine yourself by thinking you're not smart enough, connected enough or whatever you might decide makes you the wrong person to undertake your dream. Find a friend or coach to show faith in you and support you as you step into your power.

Let's pay tribute to – and take inspiration from – all spirited, open-hearted women who know and use the meaning of true power. In the words of Eleanor Roosevelt, a USA First Lady who went on to make her own mark on the world for many years after her husband Franklin's death in 1945, 'Women are like tea bags – you never know how strong they are until they get into hot water.'

This authentic power is the ability to do work or exert your will, which also includes the power of your heart, which is love. A synthesis of love and will, as we say in psychosynthesis.

Therefore, remember that taking your power is not about having power over others; it's about setting boundaries and acting on behalf of your own needs in a way that doesn't cause harm to others. In order to take your power, you have to be clear about what you feel and think of the people and situations that affect your life. You need to take time to clarify your thoughts and feelings. By not speaking up you cause yourself tremendous harm and the world loses your contribution. Even though it may be difficult, speak with a shaking voice if you have to. This happens to me when I know what I am going to say is important to me. You'll gain courage over time to always speak your mind – and your heart.

As you will have gathered, I cannot make other people see you – make you visible to all. What I hope you have learned is that when you are more at peace with yourself, stand in your own shoes, acknowledge your strengths and limitations, and you can then hold your head up, stand tall because you so appreciate yourself. Forget ageism, your time is now.

I have been inspired by all the women who have been willing to share a part of their stories as I am sure you have. Remember, at this time in history you can make a difference, whatever age you are.

Have fun, laugh, cry, take quietness for yourself. Most of all listen to yourself and enjoy being you.

Remember life is about you being visible to yourself first and then to others in the way you want to be visible for who you really are. It is about 'less *must* and more *lust*'. It is about your passion for life and living it according to that. Today be inspired to take time out for yourself to be replenished. Celebrate You for being You. Have fun.

The Visible Woman's Manifesto

As we get older, we find ourselves becoming more invisible.
Here is my manifesto. You might want to add more of your own.

I will remember that not everyone will like or approve of me

I will be aware of how I look

I will smile at people

I will worry less about what others think

I will take risks and do new things

I will do something different at least once a week

I will take time out when overwhelmed

I will listen to myself

I will remember that "being good enough" is enough

I will take note of what body is telling me

I will relieve stresses in my life

I will show love more

I will take responsibility for my feelings

I will enjoy my successes more

I will speak out

I will laugh more

I will enjoy my memories

I will remember that I can't give 100 per cent to all

I will enjoy the good people in my life

I will exercise my body and mind

I will enjoy the people I love

I will have more fun

I will retain contact only with those I want to

I will remember what I've done with my life

I will breathe in the weather

I will enjoy my quiet moments

I will enjoy life's craziness

I will be gentler with myself

101+ Things I Have Learned

(With a little help from some friends)

Everything does go south
The mirror lies
Life IS short
Traffic is getting worse
Sow your wild oats before you
    settle down
Sunshine shows up the dust
Wear what you want
Life is what you make it
HUGS are good!
Take time to just smile!
Exercise can hurt
Life isn't always fair
Do what makes you happy inside
Confidence comes with
    experience
People don't see you
Chocolate is just delicious
Don't wish for time to fly away
Laughter is the best medicine
Don't wait till you're forced into
    change
Optimism is the key to
    happiness
A bit of what you fancy does
    you good
Be there for your family and
    friends
Say NO at times too
Make the most of what you have

Take time out for yourself
Dreams can come true
Let your heart rule your head
    at times
Bad guys don't always get
    punished
Life does pass by in a flash
It's okay to relax
Take steps to deal with
    your stress
Be adventurous
The lines on the face defy the age
    felt inside
You will be envious of others
If only I knew then what
    I know now!
Be grateful for who you are
Live for the moment
Things will go wrong
That's not me in the mirror
People are good
Have confidence in yourself
Just hoover when it needs it
There is always someone
    worse off
Smile more
Regrets are the undoing of
    many things
Enjoy your money
Time does go quicker

Plans can go awry

Don't let your talents go to waste

Have an adventure a day

Sometimes it is worse than
you think

Traffic is getting worse

Appreciate yourself when young

Take more risks

Not everyone is nice

Life can be hard

There is a time for all seasons

Black can drain you

Roll with the punches

Be open

Dreams can come true

Ask for help

Wake up and smell the roses

People talk too loud on trains

Accepting change is not
always easy

Eat what you fancy now
and again

Travel does broaden the mind

Don't try to be all things to
all people

Our expectations get in
the way

Don't be rigid in your thinking

Policemen do get younger
looking

Not everyone will like you

Dancing is good exercise

Autumn leaves just keep
on falling

Hairdressers love to cut and cut

Money can bring happiness

Everyone gets stressed, it's just
human nature

You will be seen as invisible

Wear bright colours

Dance, dance, dance

Living to the best of your ability
is true

Throw out those clothes you will
never fit into

Spend more time on yourself
and your interests

Don't be so worried about what
others think

I've learned that it doesn't always
pay to try and try again

Luck has a lot to do with life, i.e.
the genes you have inherited

If only I appreciated myself
when I was younger

Do those crazy things you've
always wanted to do

Insanity is doing the same thing
over and over again

Inside me lives a slim, elegant
woman trying to get out

Try to teach your heart not to
want things it can't have

Find what triggers your stresses
and avoid them

Unexpected things can turn out
better than you can imagine

Sometimes you have to settle for
second best
Graduating through the
University of Life will give
you the edge every time
Most dry clean garments can be
done on a low wash
Life is too short to hold grudges
Switch off the TV so you can get
things done
Luck is being in the right place,
at the right time
The grass is sometimes greener
on the other side
Life isn't a trial practice – now is
for real
That second helping will go on
your hips

Childhood really is the best time
of your life
Challenge the medical team's
opinion
There's never a toilet when you
need one

Colour and greyness are both
part of life
Things will go wrong when
you're in a hurry
We're all still kids acting out our
childhood dramas
There will always be things
you'll regret
All the creams in the world won't
get rid of our wrinkles

Useful Information

Thank you for reading my book. I hope it inspires you to appreciate yourself and to rekindle your passion for life. If so, please e-mail me (irene@irenebrankin.com) and let me know. I look forward to hearing from you. Meanwhile the under mentioned may be of use to you.

Useful Websites

Carole Stacey	www.amaranti.co.uk
Amarita Vargus	www.amaritavargas.com
Susan Marr and	
Lindsay Crago	www.blueprint-tpd.co.uk
Cherie Ford	www.cherie.ford@rosemaryconley.com
Kristina Brode	www.circadian.de
Janet Derwent	www.creativegroupmeditation.org
	www.goodwillmeditation.co.uk
Helen Sieroda	www.helensieroda.co.uk
Lynne McNicholl	www.itsgood2give.co.uk
Jacqueline Burns	www.londonwritersclub.com
Maggie's Centres	www.maggiescentres.org
Carolina Welin	www.mow.se
Patrick Holford	www.patrickholford.com
PsykosynthesAkademin	www.psykosyntesakademin.se
The Psychosynthesis &	
Education Trust	www.psychosynthesis.edu
Sharon Eden	www.sharoneden.biz
Sue Donnelly	www.suedonnelly.com
Anne Welsh	www.synthesis-in-the-city.com
Suzy Greaves	www.thebigpeace.com
David Eldridge	www.twoassociates.co.uk
Jane Cooper	www.justcallmereg.com

Books I have found useful –

Assagioli, Roberto –' The Act of Will', Wildwood House, 1980

Bloom, William – 'The Endorphin Effect', Piatkus 2004

Ferucci, Piero – 'The Power of Kindness', Tarcher/Penguin 2007

Greaves, Suzy – 'Making the Big Leap', New Holland 2010

Hamilton, Dr. David – 'Why Kindness is Good for You', Hay House 2010

Holford, Patrick – 'The Feel Good Factor', Piatkus 2010

Ruddock, Jill Shaw – 'The 2nd Half of Yourself', Vermilion 2010